Cure
Your Cravings

Also by Barbara Gordon

I'm Dancing as Fast as I Can
Defects of the Heart
Jennifer Fever: Older Men, Younger Women

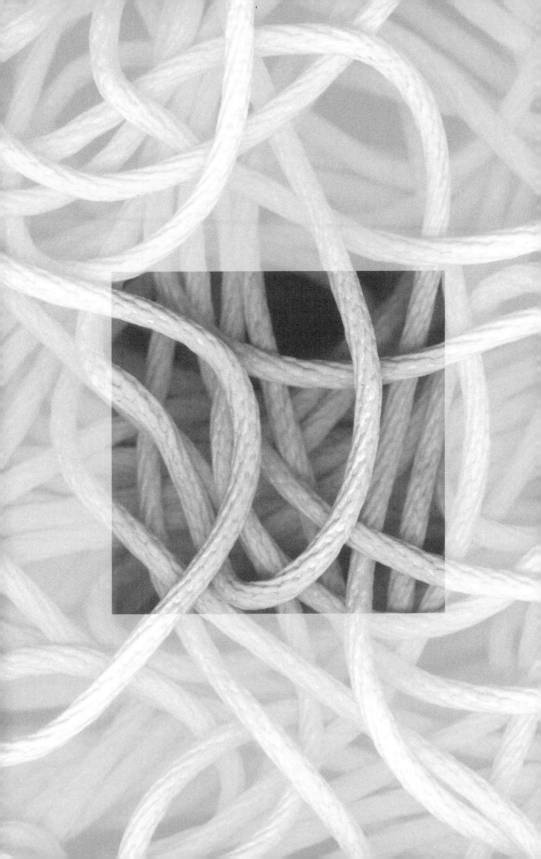

Cure

Your Cravings

Learn to Use This Revolutionary System to Conquer Compulsions

Yefim Shubentsov
and Barbara Gordon

G. P. Putnam's Sons

New York

G. P. Putnam's Sons
Publishers Since 1838
a member of
Penguin Putnam Inc.
200 Madison Avenue
New York, NY 10016

Page 170: BOO55755 Portrait of Catherine II
(1730–96) by Alexander Roslin (1718–93) (after)
Hermitage, St. Petersburg/Bridgeman Art Library
Int'l Ltd., London/New York

Published simultaneously in Canada

Library of Congress Cataloging-in-Publication Data

Shubentsov, Yefim.
Cure your cravings : learn to use this revolutionary
system to conquer compulsions / Yefim Shubentsov
and Barbara Gordon.
p.   cm.
ISBN 0-399-14398-X
1. Compulsive eating—Treatment.   2. Tobacco
habit—Treatment.   3. Self-control.   4. Addicts—
Rehabilitation.   5. Self-help techniques.
I. Gordon, Barbara, date.   II. Title
RC552.C65S45   1998   97-39194 CIP
616.85'26—dc21

Printed in the United States of America
1   3   5   7   9   10   8   6   4   2

This book is printed on acid-free paper. ∞

Book design and photo by JUDITH STAGNITTO ABBATE

Illustrations by JACKIE AHER

Author's Note

I am a healer. My training, by Western standards, is decidedly unorthodox. However, the advice I give in this book is based on my three decades of experience in using Bio Energy to treat people. My conclusions also are unusual, but not untried. Tens of thousands of people have come to see me, finding out about my Brookline office by word of mouth alone. What I say must be valid or else I wouldn't be in business!

But remember, I am not a medical doctor. I will not ask you to go against the advice of an M.D. or any other trained medical professional. I cannot ask you to alter or stop your medication regimen. Nor am I a wizard. All I know is what I've taught myself and what I've learned from my patients. But what I have learned seems to be of great help to people. But no one method works for everybody, my own included. If you apply my methods conscientiously, they should be of great help to you, too. In the pages that follow, I present my method for you.

Acknowledgments

This book would not have been possible without the help and support of my agent, Jimmy Vines. He has been a tireless advocate and a source of inspiration.

There are two other people whose assistance was invaluable. Elizabeth Himelfarb of Putnam was a constant source of targeted insights and boundless intelligence. Charles Raymond was unselfish in the extreme both with his time and encouragement.

If this book speaks to you in any way, it is because of Barbara Gordon. With dignity and poetry, she penned the lyrics to your song of freedom.

Jeremy Katz brought this project to life. Without his unstinting efforts, creative passion, and original perspective, this book would not have been possible. He shared and shaped my vision.

For my wife and son

Contents

A man encountered an angel in the village market. He asked the angel who was the greatest military leader of all time.

The angel replied, "That old man over there. He's the greatest one. He just doesn't know it."

Preface

Welcome.

Now, why are you reading this book?

Is it because you smoke?

Is it because you overeat?

Is it because you have cravings or addictions you can't control?

I know how you feel. I've seen more than 96,000 people with the same kinds of problems. And I've got news for you. I've helped nearly every last one of them.

So what can I do for you? Nothing magical, I'm afraid. No hocus pocus. I have no special gift from heaven. But I have learned from sixteen years of experience how to help people stop smoking, curb overeating, and cure their cravings.

I can help you, too—if you want to change.

Are you ready?

Cure

Your Cravings

Part 1

The Prison of Cravings and Addictions

Chapter 1

| Freedom | Awaits

To understand how I can help you and how you can help yourself, you need to understand a little about me.

In the eighteen years since I left the Soviet Union, I've learned quite a bit from the Western world. I've discovered the unmatchable feeling of freedom; I've encountered abundance that I didn't even think was possible. These past two decades have been a blur of pleasure and new experiences.

The Soviet Union was a prison. There is simply no better word for it. The freedom to live, the freedom from want that you so take for granted in the West was not merely foreign. I thought it had to be a dream.

I was determined to find out for myself.

By Soviet standards, my family and I enjoyed a comfortable living. But suspecting that freedom was out there—like a shot of color in a black-and-white world—made that comfort cold indeed.

I'll tell you a joke that was current at that time. What's the difference between freedom in the West and freedom in the Soviet Union?

In the Soviet Union you have the freedom to say whatever you want. In the West, you have freedom *after* you say whatever you want.

It's funny, in retrospect.

Our day-to-day lives were no less restricted. If I wanted to travel outside the Soviet Union, I didn't hop on a plane or catch the next train. I applied months in advance for travel papers, and even after months of waiting, more often than not, permission was denied. If I wanted to move from Moscow to St. Petersburg, I had to find someone from St. Petersburg who wanted to move to Moscow. Only then would we be allowed to move, switching one apartment for another.

The best example of all, strangely enough, happened after I left the Soviet Union. My family and I were in Rome, awaiting permission to come to the United States. While there, one of the organizations that helps to resettle Russian émigrés had provided a guide to get us acclimated. During the time we spent together, our guide, who was a dyed-in-the-wool Italian Communist, felt it wise to lecture us on the virtues of the Communist system we had fled. To him, we had left paradise on earth.

I soon found a way to show him the truth. One day, our guide, Guido, was showing us the wonders of one of Rome's many museums. While there, we encountered a group of Soviet officials on vacation being led by a real taskmaster of a tour guide. One of the Soviet officials paused at a painting to take a closer look. Before long, the rest of the group had moved on, and he was left all alone. With a glance to make sure Guido was watching, I stole up behind the lone official and in my most stern Russian, I said, "Return immediately to your group. I don't ever want to see this kind of behavior from you again." Without even a glance back to see who was talking to him, the official hurried back to his group. Anyone could see that he was terrified. He probably hasn't broken a rule in the nearly twenty years since then.

Guido was instantly cured of his love for Communism. I guess that was my first act of healing in the Western world.

I want you to understand how stout were the bars of my prison— the prison that was the Soviet Union. While there, I learned to be tough, hard enough to withstand insults and indignities on a daily basis. I learned to be clever, creative enough to find my way around or out of a problem that seemed impossible. I learned to be enduring, patient enough not to lose hope while I awaited my release.

During the time that I have lived in America, I have come to realize that many people in the free world are in a kind of prison as well. You are sitting, manacled, behind bars of your own making. Your addictions and cravings keep you walled off from the freedom that is your birthright.

Take Brian, for example. I've changed his name (as I have in this book with all of my patients). He was one of fifteen faces staring up at me during a group session on stopping smoking. After the lecture we spoke one-on-one. He was obviously overweight, and just speaking brought beads of perspiration to his forehead. And he smoked three packs a day.

Sitting across from my desk, he told me he was thoroughly dissatisfied with his life. He took little pleasure in his family because his job made him crazy. The stress of his work, and worse, failing to make as much money as he desired, left him feeling utterly despondent. At forty-one, overweight, and chain-smoking, he knew he was killing himself.

Hating his weight and his urge to overeat, despising his smoking and his craving for another cigarette, he came to me as a last resort. He had tried one diet after another, medication after medication, and every new nicotine withdrawal technique that came on the market. Nothing helped. He was trapped in his addictions, ready to throw in the towel. If that's not a prison, I don't know what is.

And then there's Lisa, a woman of average height who didn't look at all overweight. After a smoking session she came up to me and said, "I can't stop smoking. The stress from my job is too much. I work as a software engineer, and there is always some terrible deadline looming. I know that with every puff I'm poisoning my lungs. But if I don't smoke, I'll just eat and eat and eat. So I smoke, which makes me unhappy because I know it's probably killing me. But if I don't, I'll eat and get fat, which will make me even more unhappy."

Lisa feels as though she's in a windowless room with only one door. That door, she believes, leads into an even smaller and darker cell. She sees no escape.

How about Amy? A lovely woman of middle years, she carried—by American standards—a few too many pounds on her frame. (In Russia, by the way, she'd be just right!) Amy complained that her work was unfulfilling and her home life dull as well. "I'm not appreciated by my boss, my husband, or my kids," she said. "So every night I eat. I can't help it. Chocolate makes me feel better. How can I stop eating? Food is a comfort for me."

Do any of these situations sound familiar to you? I wouldn't be surprised. Rest assured you are not alone. Craving is an epidemic right now. Millions of people just like you are incarcerated against their will, held back by restraints they can't even see. But those prison bars are there all right.

Remember the Soviet Union? Let me tell you a story about my escape.

We were very worried that we wouldn't be allowed to leave at the last moment. Well, we were right to worry. It happened on our plane, but to a family we didn't know. Three black cars pulled up to the plane; KGB officers came into the plane and took the family away. We were sure they were coming back for us. But we watched through the windows as the cars drove away. And then the hum of the engines and the plane lifted off the ground. My son and my wife were clutching each other's hands. I could scarcely breathe.

After surviving life there for forty years, and then breaking free, I learned a a few things. I learned what the walls of an ideological prison are made of, and I learned how to knock them down.

Make no mistake, you are trapped by ideology as well, the politburo was my dictator—the cult of self-esteem is yours.

The KGB was the secret police terrorizing Russians—you fear the relentless dictates of public opinion.

I can lead you out of your confinement by teaching you the things I have learned. But you have to be ready. Ready to accept some things about your culture and yourself that are unpleasant. Ready to accept a new perspective that goes against much of the "wisdom" you have received. Ultimately, you have to be ready to work with me to plan your escape.

I have news for you. You aren't tough yet. You've let the prison weaken you rather than hardening your resolve. You aren't clever, either. All you see are walls where you should see crumbling mortar. And you certainly aren't patient. You want the quick fix, the magic bullet, the miracle escape to get you out of jail. Most escaped prisoners are eventually caught and brought back. Only those who demolish the building that confines them are free forever.

I come from a land of scarcity and want. A land where a bread line, as frustrating and humiliating as it was, meant that at least there was bread. Rather than diminish me, the indignities I endured strengthened my defiance. I had no choice. It was that or die—or carry out a living death. But you have let your prison sap your spirit.

I will give you a new perspective. This new way of seeing things comes from an outsider looking into your society and a former prisoner who knows what it feels like to be trapped. It will, I promise, shake up how you view the world. The oppressive dictates of public opinion will stop causing wounds. You'll soon see those messages for what they are: indignities to be shut out, then overcome. You will, I promise, become tough—impervious to the assaults of public opinion and the cult of self-esteem.

I come from a place where nothing made sense. The Soviet Union survived because its subjects abandoned their thought processes to the state. That is how every totalitarian regime operates. The rules of the game. Most people are happy to have someone else think for them. As Voltaire said, "Common sense is not so common." But if you use your God-given powers of common sense, you will see that the logic holding *your* prison walls together is brittle.

I will reignite your powers of common sense. Just as common sense showed me ways around barriers that a nonthinking person would deem impossible, your rediscovered powers of common sense will show you new solutions. A situation that seems like solitary confinement doesn't easily reveal the many exits available if you use the power of thought and creativity. Today, your problems seem to have no solution, but good old-fashioned common-sensical thinking will show you the many ways out.

I spent forty years in a country that considered standing in line to be its major form of entertainment. If I became impatient and demanded quick access to the apples, eggs, or bread, I would have succeeded only in getting myself thrown out of line. Then I'd have no hope of getting what I needed that time and quite possibly the next time as well. In the Soviet Union, patience wasn't just a virtue—it was the only option.

Every last person I have met since leaving the Soviet Union is impatient. You want the new dress now. You want to snap your fingers and have an easy answer to your problems. You need the miracle cure, the magic bullet, the instant solution. Well, it doesn't work like that. Anyone who tried to escape by fleeing over the Soviet Union's borders was either recaptured or shot. Anyone who made a spectacular jail break was killed on the run or shut away into an even tougher prison.

By rejecting the miracles being peddled to you, you can grow tougher and recapture your common sense. Then, when you leave prison, there won't be a jail to send you back to. You will have destroyed it.

It sounds almost impossible, doesn't it? It's not as bad as you think. In my Brookline office, 96,000 people have come to me to stop smoking, stop overeating, and stop craving, and in groups of fifteen, I teach them the toughness, cleverness, and patience to make it possible. I will teach them to you over the course of this book.

After the group session, I give them something else. But this has to be done one-on-one. I treat each person who comes to me using Bio Energy—an energy force I helped to discover while still behind the iron curtain. (Something good had to come from that godforsaken place.) With Bio Energy, I erase each person's craving for a cigarette, a particular binge food, or any obsession. As I said before, it's nothing magical or supernatural. It's not a gift from God. Rather, it is a power that each one of us possesses, waiting to be tapped. In this book I will show you how to turn on your own powers of Bio Energy—your newly discovered sixth sense.

I will introduce you to a power you never knew you had, but through these pages I cannot erase your craving for a particular thing with *my* Bio Energy. When you activate your power of Bio Energy, you will be able to explore your own healing energy. I will show you that you possess a truly new way to perceive the physical world around you. It's taken me more than three decades of study to learn to be a "human eraser." And I will open the door to this new power to you.

Just think, if you discover a totally new way to learn about the physical world, is it so strange to think that you could learn to perceive the social world differently? It shouldn't be difficult to realize that the world of cravings and addictions—a world much less concrete than this book or your chair—can be explored in a much different light.

At the end of this book, you'll realize that you have a power you haven't dreamed of. Doesn't it stand to reason that you have the power to break out of your addictions and cravings and just don't realize it? At the end of this book, you'll know that you have the power to destroy your addictions and cravings, but just like having your powers of Bio Energy, you just didn't know it.

Every prisoner who makes a successful escape comes to realize he has untapped powers. I have a favorite story that will help me make this point. I often tell this to my patients in Brookline. Let me share it with you:

A man encounters an angel in a small village market. The man, believing the angel knows everything about a person, good or bad, asks the angel, "Who is the greatest military leader, the greatest warrior in the world?"

The angel, pointing to an elderly man sitting crouched over a small bag of tomatoes at the far end of the market, replies, "There. That old man is the greatest warrior of all time. He could be. He just doesn't know it. Yet."

Now you know you have untapped powers to cure your cravings and addictions forever. If you *desire* to change, the prison of your smoking, of your overeating, of your cravings is beginning to collapse. If you are reading this book, your prison is formed of rotting walls and crumbling mortar. You have the power to wreck its walls once and for all.

Allow me to tell you one more story. After I filled out the application for my family and me to leave the country, the official studied our papers and then asked me with a puzzled expression, "Why do you want to leave?"

I couldn't take such a question seriously. I replied, "You'll never understand."

He looked at me sharply and again asked, "Why?"

"Because you had to ask," I told him. "That's why you'll never understand."

Not only did the Soviet official not want to leave prison, he did not even realize that he was trapped. He couldn't even fathom why anyone would want to leave so "perfect" a life.

Remember that poor family I told you about—the one that was whisked off the plane by the KGB and back into the prison of the Soviet Union? That can happen to you—a bump in the road—a promotion denied, a fight with your spouse, a dwindling bank account. But my family and I stayed on the plane. And so can you.

There may be those around you who don't need a KGB to keep them in prison. They enslave themselves to their own addictions. They may be unwilling to leave their addictions and cravings behind. Why? They may be so settled that they view the walls as protection rather than confinement and their addictions as comforts, not assaults. Too often people feel safe and secure in the known, in the familiar. They are afraid of the unknown. Afraid of what escape to freedom may be like.

You may even feel that way. But should the moment come when the protective walls feel menacing and the addictions and cravings feel more like chains than comforts, then you have it within you to be free. If not, then put this book down. You are not ready.

Freedom awaits.

Are you ready?

Remember Amy? Her nightly bingeing is now under control. She glows with self-confidence and doesn't worry about whether she's appreciated or not. She knows full well her own worth.

All Amy had needed was toughness. She had to learn to reject society's judgments and standards and not to rely on the crutch of low self-esteem. Her weight loss was for herself—*her* health, *her* sense of well-being—not to gain anyone else's approval.

Remember Lisa? Well, common sense took hold in her. She came to understand that it was crazy to kill herself over her job. She wrote me a letter, saying, "Stress is a killer, and smoking is, too. And those are two things I no longer have time for. Smoking is a toxic way of dealing with stress. I thought about what you said and the techniques you taught me. So when I begin to feel stress, I remember that it's deadly. I lose twice for every brain cell that dies—once when it dies and once for the time in the future when I'll need it. And I decided it was time to stop killing myself to make my boss rich. So I don't smoke anymore and I haven't gained an ounce!"

I had known all along that with just a bit of common-sense analysis and creative insight, she would see the light under the doors that weren't there before.

Lisa is not the only former patient I have heard this story from. Maybe if you follow the program I'll outline for you in this book, if you resolve to destroy your personal prison, I'll hear a similar tale from you, too.

My peculiar Russian fix on the world has caused me to be dubbed the "Mad Russian." But I see that as a badge of honor because it is precisely my unorthodox ideas and methods that have been of so much help to so many people.

How I've helped 96,000 people in their battles against chronic cravings and addictions is what these pages will teach you.

The program I offer here is the same as the one I teach to the thousands of people who come from all over the world to my Brookline, Massachusetts, office.

Much of what I have to say will go against the grain of what you have heard or read on the subject of cravings and addictions. At times you will find my advice unconventional. Unconventional, yes. But not untried.

For example, I don't have to tell you about the evils of smoking. Or that being overweight can endanger your health. I don't tell it to my patients in Brookline, and I don't have to tell it to you. You know this already, or else you wouldn't be reading this book.

My methods have helped large numbers of people. If you can stand to see the walls of your prison come down as you watch some popular myths blown to pieces, I think you will find my methods working for you.

But I've got news for you. Unlike everything you've heard before, this works.

If you follow my advice, the weight you lose on my program is gone for good, unlike the yo-yo pounds you've had before. The cigarette habit you drop won't reappear as it has in the past, the next time you're feeling stressed out or upset. The cravings for either cigarettes or food you've been battling will be broken once and for all, not just placed on hold. And with my method, you won't gain weight when you stop smoking.

Why am I certain that nothing else out there works? Because I know that you've tried one system after another, and you're still reading this book.

Why am I so certain my method works as a permanent solution—that the pounds stay off, that cigarettes stay unsmoked not just for a week or a month, but permanently? Because I've treated thousands of patients, and every single one of them has been told he or she is welcome to come back—free of charge—for another treatment, a discussion, or any support I can offer for the rest of my life in this profession. If even 10% of my patients came back, I wouldn't need a waiting room—I'd need a stadium!

I'll show you why they don't have to come back and how a number of people I've treated have successfully triumphed over addictions and problems that have haunted their lives.

So can you. You are acquiring the weapons to become free of the prison. You can use them to begin to change your life.

Oh, yes. Remember Brian? He came to my office recently as I was wrapping up for the day. Bounding through the door, he embraced me and handed over a huge bouquet of flowers. Honestly, I didn't recognize him, so much had he changed. He was trim and in obvious good health as he ticked off the ways his life was changed. He no longer smoked, his marriage was on better ground, he had shed all the excess weight, and he felt better than he had in years. Moreover, he had redoubled his efforts to earn the salary he wanted.

His smoking, his weight, his family, his job—not knowing where to begin, frustrated by the tangle of vices and problems that fed each other, he'd all but given up. But he had lacked only a single weapon. Patience, the will to find the *right* fix, not the quick fix. Endurance carried him through.

Only after he left did I look at the card. Written down was the exact phrase I had said to him two years before.

"Your success is my success."

And that, by the way, is how I end every one of my sessions.

Chapter 2

The Religion of Self-esteem/
The Virtue of Toughness

People are the same everywhere, so I think Russians aren't so different from people in the West. But even after eighteen years of living in America, there is one difference I still find most intriguing.

What is that difference?

The style of life.

For sure, as Westerners, you have a better style of life than people in any other part of the world. And it's only natural that your better style of life has shaped how you approach living. It can affect both your fears and your expectations—often in very unexpected ways.

Since leaving the Soviet Union, I have had the opportunity to get an intimate picture of how that grander style of life affects the behavior of many free people. I think, in some ways, it has made you, shall I say, a bit more spoiled than people in Russia. It has given many of you a sense of entitlement that only makes you weaker.

Based on my own experience, meeting thousands of people in my Brookline clinic, I have seen for myself how this weakness, this vulnerability can undermine the inner core of toughness that each of us needs to live independently.

I know all too well how priceless is the sense of being in charge of your own life. I also know it requires that your hard kernel of toughness remain intact. If it is intact, you will always have a clear sense of exactly who you are. If it erodes, your power to be free dissolves with it.

The patience I told you about earlier, the cleverness so essential to your personal freedom is demolished when your core of inner toughness is weakened by this vulnerability to entitlement.

With a sense of personal freedom—nourished by patience, toughness, and creativity—your life can have a solid foundation. Without it, I will show you how this vulnerability can become the foundation for a life of enslavement, of a life lived behind invisible prison walls.

More than anything else, this vulnerability has made you receptive to the whispers of propaganda.

Yes, like the Soviet Union, the Western world has its own forms of propaganda.

When I lived in the Soviet Union, the truth was manipulated by the politburo to keep the Russian people locked in the prison of a totalitarian state, compelled to live in a land that demanded conformity of thought and the slavish acceptance of the rules.

But now, almost twenty years later, I understand clearly that the governments of the free world don't dictate to their subjects in the same way.

But I do understand—because I see day after day—that many of you still act as if you have no choice. You accept wholeheartedly an entire set of rules that are not forced on you by your government or by anyone else. You unquestioningly adhere to many ideas that you follow scrupulously, even blindly. Some of this conformity is harmless, but some of it eats away your personal freedom by asking you to march, lockstep, to the rhythm of the same repetitive theme, in your quest for the same impossible ideal. And no ideal is more corrupting than the misguided notion of self-esteem as a cure-all.

The Dictatorship of Self-esteem

As someone who actually experienced life under a dictatorship for almost forty years, I can see that the quest for self-esteem has become the dictatorship under which many of you live. I can also understand why.

The gods of self-esteem offer a host of false promises, and their apostles have effectively spread the word: miracles do exist. And self-esteem has become the free world's late-twentieth-century miracle. Because with it, you no longer need to take responsibility for your actions. The cult of self-esteem eliminates the necessity for responsible behavior.

Like an essential vitamin or mineral missing in a person's bloodstream, the apostles of this false god propagate the notion that all anyone needs to cure any problem—craving or addiction, emotional or physical—is a shot of self-esteem.

Eager to find a scapegoat for their problems, longing for an understanding of what drives them to self-defeating behavior, or unwilling to face reality, worshipers venerate the cult of self-esteem. A true religion, Christianity, says that Jesus died for people's sins to be *forgiven*. But this other cult says that if you have a lack of self-esteem, your sins are *excused*. Self-esteem, like any cult, is a false god, as false as the promises it offers its followers; as false as the excuses and alibis used by its adherents to explain away their self-defeating behavior. The religion of self-esteem doesn't offer solutions—it offers the status quo.

The Soviet Union had the KGB to enforce the rules the politburo designed.

In the West, public opinion is the enforcer. It is the secret police that patrols your self-imposed prison of addictions and cravings, and it is the army that commands you to obey the rules.

If America's military is feared, it is because of its potential power and its willingness to fight. It is the same with the army of public opinion. Its authority is based on the power that conformity and "group-think" has over all of us. And we all know just how eager public opinion—a.k.a. "everybody" or "they"—is to enlist us. Anger the army of public opinion, and you will be excluded from the group.

But you are about to learn that your fear is misplaced. Public opinion cannot ostracize you. In fact, public opinion has no real authority over you whatsoever. Its power is an illusion—just as the power of the Soviet state proved to be an illusion once the people challenged it. Once you rise against public opinion, it will crumble.

One of the weapons of the army of public opinion is its insistence on your accepting unrealistic expectations about yourself. By imposing false ideals and impossible standards, public opinion fortifies the cult of self-esteem.

Let me show you how this insidious pattern develops. By providing you with impossible goals, public opinion makes it all too easy to feel defeated and thus achieve nothing at all. Then, public opinion makes it a snap to return to your bad habits and self-defeating behavior.

For example, like many of my patients, after learning about the success or the glamour or the achievements of someone you know or even a total stranger, you may tell yourself: "My life will never live up to my expectations. I'll never be like *that,* or I'll never have *this,* or be able to do *that.* In fact, what's the point of ever changing, since I'll always be found wanting. So I have good reason to binge or smoke or whatever. At least I enjoy that."

You can also see how that creates fertile territory for scapegoating and how it gives you license to indulge in all sorts of terrible behavior. You can see how unrealistic goals lead back into our old friend self-esteem. It's the perfect excuse! This is how the army of public opinion keeps you locked in the oppressive world of addictions and cravings.

This toxic combination can create a prison that is entirely self-imposed. If you listen to the propaganda, if you fall under the spell of these ruling passions, you can become trapped in a prison of the self, a prison you have built yourself, brick by brick.

This prison may not be as visible as the armed guards who patrolled the borders of the Soviet Union. But from what I have witnessed, it seems just as secure.

I refused to allow the enforcing army to get to me when I lived in the Soviet Union. I couldn't accept the daily barrage of propaganda or the dogma that we were expected to swallow. I didn't understand the Russians who could accept it and who lived with its restrictions. But I do understand how easy it is for Westerners to allow themselves to be controlled by public opinion and become devoted followers of the cult of self-esteem. I want to show you how to escape from this cult and the control it has over your life.

If you are one of those who are held in its grip, in order to free yourself from the vise-like hold it has over your life, you must have a plan. Vital to this plan is recognizing that the essential ingredient of conventional wisdom is an unblinking acceptance of the dogma of self-esteem. It is the god we are all asked to serve.

Self-esteem is not the powerful, life-enhancing elixir it's cracked up to be. It is not an essential nutrient. It is not a requirement for success. Rather, it is the *result of* success. Feeling entitled to self-esteem takes away all the toughness that comes from having *earned* it.

In order to break free of the prison of addictions and cravings, you need to mobilize all your powers.

To do this you must free yourself first from the tyranny of public opinion and and say good-bye to the gods of self-esteem.

Let me give you a perfect example of the absurd but tyrannical power public opinion holds in our society and how it helps to fortify the cult of self-esteem.

I read in a magazine article that, for example, 26 million American people who have diplomas from high school don't know how to read or write. I once spoke to a schoolteacher in America about this, asking her, "You give diplomas to twenty-six million idiots who after twelve years in school can't read or write! How can this happen?"

She said, "You talk like a Russian."

I said, "I am a goddamned Russian."

She explained it this way: "If you pass the whole class from one

grade together, and one guy has to stay a second year, and sometimes another year, because he's stupid or lazy, he'll lose self-
esteem."

I thought, marvelous! "Are you saying," I asked the teacher,
"that this means that it's better to have twenty-six million complete idiots with self-esteem, than to have twenty-six million
well-educated people without?"

She nodded, "Yes. American public opinion says that it's better."

"Then that American way is stupid," I said.

Now don't get me wrong. I am not really a Mad Russian. I have
nothing against self-esteem. But it seems to me that self-esteem
doesn't exist by itself. Self-esteem is not like blue eyes or blond
hair. Unlike the gene that determines whether you're dark or fair,
tall or short, there is no gene for self-esteem.

You are not born with a reserve of self-esteem. Self-esteem
must be earned. If you do everything well, you get self-esteem. If
you do everything terribly, you're not supposed to get it. Self-
esteem is the *result* of living well—not the prerequisite.

Let me give you another example. When I watch television—
which admittedly is not often, but when I do—I experience the
feeling of a person who's arrived here from another planet, not just
from another country. I can see why so many people are so easily
confused and unable to break free of their addictions and cravings.
I can also understand why they offer the same excuses or rationales
for behavior that they know is bad for their health.

Self-esteem has become a cliché. It has become an international
mantra, chanted a hundred times a day in the media. Self-esteem
is confirmed daily as the prerequisite for success in the popular wis-

dom spun out by the daytime talk shows. It is worshiped by millions of devoted followers of what passes for self-help books. It is the hidden message in commercials as well as made-for-TV movies.

Clean clothes, sparkling windows? Signs of healthy self-esteem. Teenagers dabbling with drugs or promiscuous sex? Lack of self-esteem.

The armies of popular opinion are everywhere, selling it like a miracle drug. Like an injection of B-12 for energy, or insulin for a diabetic, public opinion insists that if you are simply given a blast of self-esteem, all of your problems will vanish. Instantly.

This notion has been greedily lapped up by people starving for an explanation for their problems. Whatever the problem—be it overeating or smoking, emotional or physical, bad behavior or downright criminality—the diagnosis is the same: self-esteem deficiency.

I can easily understand why this happens. I see it everyday in my office. People are eager, often desperate, to break free of their addictions and cravings. When they fail, naturally they are just as eager, just as desperate, for an explanation or a rationale for behavior they *know* is harmful. They are particularly vulnerable and receptive to any explanation that will let them off the hook.

The oppressive armies of public opinion are clever. They know just how to feed that hunger for an explanation. But like the empty calories consumed by the junk-food addict, public opinion only feeds a hungry public empty promises.

And the result? People remain imprisoned, manacled to their addiction.

The popular wisdom goes even further. It proclaims that *all* self-indulgent behavior—smoking, overeating, and even abusive behavior, behavior that hurts not only yourself but others—is easily explainable.

Whether it's because of the damage wrought by an unloving parent or the injury inflicted by an overadoring one, the cause is the same: lack of self-esteem. Whether you endured the trauma of being lost among too many siblings or the terror of being an only child, whether you are unable to feel anger, or suffer the consuming rage of feeling too much of it, the problem is—quite simply—a lack of self-esteem. A little more self-esteem and—poof!—everything's solved.

I admire so much about the West—the freedom you have—the opportunity to control your own life, to improve your standard of living. But my admiration doesn't blind me from seeing how those same comforts and opportunities can create an environment that allows the cult of self-esteem to flourish.

In the West, where you are more comfortable, where more people have a good life—an extraordinarily good life compared to that of the average Russian—perhaps you don't want that good life jolted by a dose of disturbing reality.

You don't want to hear anything unpleasant, even from your teacher. Or your doctor. You don't want to hear about discipline and self-control. You don't want to recognize the fact that *you* are the only one with power over your life.

In short, you don't really want to be tough.

What I tell my patients is what I tell you: this attitude restricts your power over your own lives. This way of thinking keeps you imprisoned in a dark, windowless room.

> **Feeling powerless, but blameless.**

Don't allow yourself to live under the dictatorship of self-esteem. I lived under a dictatorship for most of my life, and, trust me, it can destroy you in the end.

Let me give you an example of how public opinion feeds your unrealistic expectations. From your doctor you want diets that promise miracles, lifetime guarantees of thinness, recipes for hunger-free and painless methods of weight control. Even though you must know somewhere deep inside that the minute you go off the diet, the minute you live without the restrictions imposed by any diet, the minute you stop exercising, you will gain it all back.

To blame doctors alone for this situation misses the point. Like many patients susceptible to the passions and rages of popular opinion, you often *demand* these miracles from your doctor.

Demanding miracles, you want to block out the hard truths that your doctor tries to tell you. For instance, when your doctor tells you that smoking is killing you, that isn't public opinion; that's a medical fact. If your doctor warns you that being overweight can damage your heart or lead to diabetes, that, too, is a medical fact.

But often you blunt the force of the doctor's argument. In a way, you seduce the doctor, just as you have been seduced by the army of public opinion. For instance, you may tell your doctor your life is so empty, or you feel so unappreciated, you can't stop eating. You promise the doctor that as soon as your self-esteem has improved, as soon as you get through these bumps in the road, you'll go on a diet or tackle giving up cigarettes.

After hearing your heartfelt excuses for behavior that is obviously dangerous to your health, it is often difficult for many doctors to insist that you heed their warnings and shape up. Why?

The answer is simple. Many doctors are card-carrying members of the cult of self-esteem. They're vulnerable to the same forces that have assailed you. They too can be ruled by the enforcers of the army of public opinion.

Too often, they are willing to agree when a patient tells them self-esteem is the problem. Their compassion, regrettably, only re-inforces the problem. That only seals the door to the prison of your addiction more securely.

It's much harder for a doctor to tell a person, "You are responsible for your misery. You aren't overeating because of a lack of self-esteem. You aren't smoking because of a self-esteem deficiency. Self-esteem is not a goal; it is a result."

I repeat,

> # Self-esteem is not a goal; it is a result.

This is what I was taught in school, and doctors in the Soviet Union went to the same schools as I did and were taught as I was taught. While I abhor almost all of the philosophy and the dogma and indoctrination imposed by Soviet Communism, in this one sense, I agree with what Russian doctors were taught. Namely, tell it straight, the way I'm telling you, the way I think it's better for you. But from what I've observed, some Western doctors try to please the patient. They don't want to make their patients feel responsible for their overeating, or for almost any problem, for that matter.

I hear it in my office everyday. One patient, Gina, told me, "I know why I overeat. The reason I overeat is because I had an impoverished emotional life as a child. Food was my only comfort then, just as it is today."

My first instinct was to say to her, "Bullshit! Now you are thirty-five. The past is gone. It's history. If you continue to talk about it, you'll have no future. You are old enough to be a responsible person. You should take command. Discipline and self-control are not genetic. You have to work at it."

Toughness, patience, creativity—these are the essential weapons that helped Gina, and they can help you to open that one door that leads to freedom.

Developing Toughness

So, what can you do?

I know I shouldn't be so damned Russian. Some people don't like to be talked to like that. People come for my help, not for me to show how them how they conspire to keep themselves locked in the world of their addictions.

But as someone who escaped from a land of tyranny to a land of freedom, I find it difficult not to say what I see. And what I see, time and again, is that too many people can't escape tyranny of another sort. The tyranny of addiction and craving. But it's tyranny, just the same. What I offer my patients is what I offer in these pages—the blueprint, the plan for escape.

Today, I realize I can help without being so damned Russian. I admit, it was difficult to change my approach. You grow up in a country, you grow up with its history, its traditions, its culture—everything.

But Russian or not, I still believe that people should not be infantalized and indulged. That way, they will never solve their problems. I know the most important thing in life is what we're thinking—not what we have, not what we will have, not what we possibly can't afford to have, but what we're thinking about.

> **W**hat you're thinking, this is what your life will be.

If you make this thought your own, it will become one of your most effective weapons in breaking out of the prison of public opinion and self-esteem. If you replace the tenets of public opinion with these words, they will guide you like a ray of light filtering through a crack in your prison door. With the help of that flash of light, the glow of the insight, you will be ready to receive the other weapons that will help you weaken the foundation and ultimately crumble the walls of your prison.

Consider the opposite philosophy, the abuse excuse. This is one of the favorite apostles of the gods of self-esteem. The abuse excuse provides a means to justify your cravings such as overeating and smoking. In fact, it is used to explain away all kinds of self-destructive behavior.

If you find yourself imprisoned in the dark cell of addiction and cravings, I promise you, the abuse excuse will not help you. It will only keep you confined in a dark, joyless place.

For example, if you cling to the notion that emotional injuries inflicted on you during childhood, or a current emotional problem, are the reasons why you overeat or smoke or find yourself craving and bingeing, you're writing a self-fulfilling prophecy.

In my view, neither the love you lacked in the past nor the love you miss in your current life has anything to do with the cravings that torment you today. But if you tell yourself a story, you'll soon believe it. So if you tell yourself that it's old pains—the scar tissue of past emotional injuries—that give you stress and the unstoppable craving for food, you will believe it. And you will stay locked in your windowless chamber.

Similarly, like my former patient, Lisa, if you tell yourself that the stress you are experiencing at home and at work is the source of all your pain, you will believe it, and that will become the target of your blame. My point is: neither past nor present emotional pain or stress means you're doomed to live a life of constant cravings, whether it be smoking or chronic overeating.

> **So you think,
> so shall your life be.**

If you tell yourself your life must remain a prison, so shall your life be. And you will never be free. Here is a perfect example of what a powerful message is contained in those words. When Napoléon Bonaparte died, in his diary it was written down, "In all my entire life, I cannot find more than six happy days."

Imagine! We're talking about one of the most famous people in history—about one of the most powerful people in history. A man who lived for fifty-two years. At the end, he could say that in all his years on this planet, he had only six happy days.

Why? I believe the reason is that, incredibly enough, he was never satisfied with what he had. It is the best example of my philosophy. Napoléon had everything one can possibly imagine, more than you can possibly imagine, and still he could say he enjoyed only six happy days.

Another example: today, according to international opinion,

the best style of life is in Scandinavian countries. In Sweden, by the way, nobody ever asks, "Do you have a vacation house?" They ask, "*Where* is your vacation house?"

Yet Sweden has one of the highest rates of suicide in the world. Why? Because a majority of the Swedish people think they had miserable lives before, and they still think they have miserable lives. This is not because they *really* have such miserable lives. Other people from other countries such as India, for example, cannot even dream about such styles of life as the Scandinavians enjoy.

If Napoléon could say he had only six happy days, and the Scandinavians, with all their gains as a society in terms of quality of life and economic security, can have the highest suicide rate, what does that tell us?

> # What you're thinking;
> ## this is what your life will be.

I know that at first it's easier to say those words than to truly absorb them and make them your own. We live in a world where we are constantly bombarded with messages. The air is crowded with seductive suggestions telling you how to think, how you should look, and, worst of all, how you should feel and how you should *be*. Sometimes it can be difficult to tune out the world and know what *you* think. Yet it's crucial to your freedom to separate your own thoughts from the babble filling the air. It's crucial because in order to hone your creativity, develop your innate cleverness, and sharpen your common sense, you have to be 100% sure of what *you* believe.

Let me give you a parallel from my own life when I still lived in the Soviet Union. Each of us knew that a small group of people—the politburo—created the laws that determined what we could do and not do, what we could say or not say, where we could go or not go.

I find it amazing that today in America, we live in a world where small groups of ten or twelve people are used by giant corporations as samples of the opinions of the much wider world. That small group, sometimes called a focus group, often provides the seed of an idea that will, in time, be added to the huge arsenal of public opinion.

I know you have to be superhuman not to internalize some of these messages, not to accept them as the standards by which you judge yourself. This is important because some of the messages you receive are facts, containing truths that can save your life. As I've already told you, when medical science tells you that smoking is toxic, you should believe it. When doctors demonstrate time and again that carrying excess weight endangers your health, you should believe that, too.

But if you absorb *all* the messages from the media about how you should be and how you should feel, what you should think and what you should not, you are losing touch with your own precious common sense.

If you ignore the message and the messenger, you will find the way to unlock the door that can lead you to freedom.

The Blueprint

What can you do? As someone who has escaped from a dark and terrible place, I must remind you that you must toughen up! You must be tough and persistent. Begin to arm yourself, gather the weapons that will help you shake the very foundation of the prison walls that encircle you. Willfully, consciously, ignore the messages being pandered to you. Search for the poison behind the promise. Rebel against the empty calories in the food public opinion serves up to nurture your soul. Recognize those vaunted wizards of all-knowing wisdom for what they are. They are not people whose opinions "really count." They are a small but dedicated group who have one goal. To sell you a bill of goods. To control how you think. To inspire what you want and don't want.

You must consciously ignore the messages being peddled by the purveyors of mass culture. At first, it will be difficult, even unnatural. But before long, you'll be amazed. What does this remind you of? It reminds me of the politburo, the small but dedicated group that ruled my life for forty years.

If I could throw off the myths propagated by the Communists, you can ignore the myths propagated by public opinion. If I could block out the Soviet propaganda mill constantly spinning out a fairy tale about how wonderful life was in the Soviet Union, you can see that the myths of public opinion are simply that—myths. Whatever the myth—whether it is "Being skinny means being beautiful" or "If you had a cruel and unloving father, you're doomed to being overweight and miserable"—remember it is only propaganda. One highly effective piece of propaganda I hear in my office on a regular basis goes something like this:

I might as well indulge my craving. I've been divorced for years and can't meet anyone. I am alone; work sucks. At least smoking [or chocolates or pizza or french fries] gives me some pleasure in my life.

It can be any of a hundred other popular myths—all are possible for you to overcome once you've toughened up. Once you do, the foundation for the prison structure is weakened and the walls of your prison begin to crumble.

If I could evade the KGB, you can outsmart the secret police that is public opinion.

As I've said before, thousands of people visit my office for help in giving up their addiction to smoking or food or some other craving that is making their lives a misery.

I show them, as I'm showing you, that self-esteem is as dangerous a cult as there is. It suckers you in and urges you to kill yourself, slowly, by helping you keep those self-defeating, self-harming behaviors alive.

I hope you are good and mad now—furious at the system that has set us up for so much pain.

Well, I have another hard truth for you.

You are just as much to blame.

This is one of the main principles of my philosophy, vital to my method of treating cravings:

You are addicted to public opinion and self-esteem. Those are the first cravings that you must break.

I know that this seems a damn near-impossible task. But, I promise you that all it requires is a little attitude adjustment. I'll give you an example.

I remember my former patient, Brian, complaining about hearing on a radio talk show that until his self-esteem was enhanced, he was doomed to being overweight. This made him feel he was destined to feel like he was living on the sidelines of his own life.

What I told him can be a useful weapon as you make your plans for escape.

"Would you put up with some punk telling you how to run your life?" I asked him. "Well, popular opinion is that punk and self-esteem is the false promise—the glittery but illusory piece of gold he serves up to deflect blame."

When you hear this message, like Brian, you can learn to see it as the insult that it truly is.

We must see these as the insults they are. No one can determine what we will do and who we will be.

You must tune out these messages, just as you tune out static on a radio or the piercing sound of an electric saw breaking through the silence of a peaceful Sunday afternoon.

When you hear them, when the slogans and the mantras and the false promises of the gods of self-esteem fill the air, recognize them for what they are: insults to your intelligence.

Then you can train yourself to simply change the subject. Think about it—you do this every day about far less important things. Tell yourself, "If I listen to this mumbo jumbo, if I excuse my bingeing or my smoking, I will only be adding more bricks to the walls of my prison." Don't dwell on it, but move on. By doing this, you deny them life, you deprive these messages of the oxygen necessary to blossom in your mind. I'll teach you a good technique for changing the subject in chapter 9.

Once you learn to ignore the misguided dictates of the culture of self-esteem, once you learn to shut them out, you'll begin to toughen up.

I know it's difficult to ignore public opinion and treat it like an insult. The messages surround you. They ooze into your very pores. It feels as though those messages are a part of you—that they are what *you* think as well.

They're not.

You know your own mind. You know what your core values and beliefs are, and you know they don't change.

Do you like the color red? I bet you liked it last year as well. You probably even liked it when you were a kid. But the fashion industry—another outlet for public opinion—might say red is a bad color this year. Green is in, and too bad if you don't like it. Too bad if you look like a worm in it. You *will* like green.

Beginning to see the difference?

What about food? Do you like red meat? Well, public opinion used to say that it's terrible to eat meat. It would kill you surer than walking in front of a bus. Now there are ads on television saying how wonderful it is. Have meat every night for dinner! You know the truth. It's the same as you've always known. Don't eat a side of beef for lunch, but enjoy an occasional hamburger or steak with a clear conscience.

Public opinion is always variable. You will remain vulnerable as long as you listen to its voices.

How are you supposed to be tough if you are blown around with every shifting wind? That is what will happen as long as you think public opinion knows better than you do.

But how do you know that what you think is right? You won't until you compare the seductions of public opinion with your own truths. Think about it. How many times has public opinion let you down in the past?

Body type, for example. First, you were supposed to be round. Then you had to be straight. Then you had to be skinny. Then emaciated. And now? Emaciated and round. It's absurd. Only you know what your body should look like when you are healthy.

Toughness comes from scar tissue. In the Soviet Union, we had to develop scar tissue. The horror of World War II, the destruction of our glorious culture and art, the constant threat of the

KGB, the relatives locked away in gulags, and countless other wounds. We had to develop scar tissue or bleed to death.

Public opinion is no less harmful. It's wounded you time and again. When you accept its insults, it draws blood. If you ignore these shifting strains of public opinion and listen to the dictates of your own mind, the scar tissue begins to form. Over time, the scar tissue will build up and you'll have a tough hide. Ignoring public opinion will become easier and easier because no insult will be able to penetrate your toughened exterior.

That is toughness. And that is what you must develop.

Destroying your prison will be dangerous and difficult. You'll need every bit of toughness you can get.

The Rules of Engagement

For every major battle, the military designs a plan called the "rules of engagement." Make no mistake about it. Breaking out of this prison will be a war.

Many of you already know Sun-tzu's famous admonition: "Know your enemy." The enemy is what you've spent this past chapter learning. Your adversaries aren't just cravings and addictions. No, you are in a holy war against the cult of self-esteem, fighting its army of public opinion.

Sun-tzu also says something less well known: "To leave the field of battle victorious, you must know your enemy *and* yourself."

So, before we make war against cravings—food, cigarettes, or whatever craving you're trying to conquer, whatever craving has made you feel enslaved and powerless—let me share with you the two caveats that I always mention in my office sessions.

First, I will make you a promise. I will help you lose weight. But I must warn you, if you're losing this weight to impress others, or because of what others will think, I promise you will never be free. Or happy. Why? The answer is based on my belief that if you're concerned about public opinion, you'll never really break out of your prison.

Whatever it is that you want to accomplish, whether it's losing weight or stopping smoking or curing some other craving, if you wish to do this because you believe that public opinion places a premium on skinniness, or socially disapproves of smokers, then I can promise you that almost nothing you do will make you happy.

That is because if public opinion is the measure by which you judge yourself, you will always find something else about yourself that doesn't measure up to what public opinion regards as admirable, attractive, acceptable—the list is endless.

The West didn't fight Communism by adopting the Soviet Union's belief system. So why should *you* listen to the words of the enemy? Public opinion cannot hold sway in the minds of those who are battling their craving for food and who are struggling to achieve weight loss that is both permanent and manageable.

Consider the following example: imagine that you were stranded in the middle of the ocean, and you found your way to a deserted island. After searching all over this island, imagine that you discovered you were totally, I mean completely, alone. You realized that no one would ever see you again. And also imagine that you discovered that this was an island blessed with lush vegetation—with enough fruit and nuts and vegetables—to last you a lifetime. But remember nobody would ever see you again. Now, please, consider the answer to this question very carefully:

Would you try to lose weight, for God's sake?

Of course, I'm not suggesting that you should live your entire life as if you're stranded on a deserted island, never to see another human being again for as long as you live. But I *am* saying

Don't lose weight or anything else to impress others. Or to win the love or admiration of others.

Why? The majority of people are motivated by self-interest. If you lose weight, you won't necessarily win the love or admiration of others. You will inspire their envy or jealousy.

If you want to lose weight to feel better, however, for your health, for your heart, to be able to climb a flight of stairs without feeling breathless and exhausted, or to feel good when you look in the mirror, for *yourself,* then fine. I'll show you how to accomplish your goal. If you want to stop smoking because you are short of breath, because your morning cough is becoming chronic, I'll show you the plan to escape.

But here's my second caveat. I have a favorite saying: A skinny cow is not a gazelle. What I mean by that is, being skinny doesn't mean you're beautiful. Throughout my years in the United States, I have met hundreds of women who have struggled endlessly to be skinny. They have bought the nonstop message of the armies of public opinion.

I tell them what I will now tell you. I've never seen one man who liked skinny women. If you're uncertain about this, just look at any sex magazine that men read, and I'm sure you won't find one skinny woman. In fact, I know plenty of men who like *any* woman, but I never met one man who liked *skinny* women. So don't drive yourself crazy with your obsession with weight. It won't help you lose; it won't give you self-esteem; it'll only make you crazy.

These are, I know, unconventional observations, particularly coming from someone who's about to help you conquer your cravings and lose weight.

Unconventional, possibly. But useful? Absolutely.

Remember Amy? Feeling unappreciated at home and work, she had nightly binges of consoling herself with chocolates. When she ate the chocolate she felt better, but the next day as she struggled to get into a dress or wasn't able to button a pair of slacks, she was furious at herself. At a loss, frustrated by an apparent lack of choices, she felt imprisoned by her own cravings.

Months after our session, Amy and I saw each other at a concert in Boston. She looked wonderful! Trim, happy, confident. She took me aside and poured out her thoughts, "Now, I see it clearly. Life cannot be lived without disappointments. And you were right about one thing. I had bought into an impossible standard for myself. When my life didn't turn out that way, when it didn't match the pictures I had in my head of what my life *should* be, I took solace in food.

"I knew the nightly chocolate binges were making me unhappy. What's more, they weren't good for me. But when I tore into the box each night, I told myself that since I couldn't have what I wanted in life, what was the point of not eating chocolate? Since no one appreciated me, I thought I might as well have the joy of my chocolates. At least I enjoyed that.

"And it became like circles within circles. On and on. Until I came to your session. Once you made me face the facts, I saw the pile of excuses I had concocted to justify my nightly binges. That's when everything began to change."

For Amy, that was the moment when the walls of her prison had begun to crumble. When we first met, Amy and I had discussed that vicious cycle one-to-one. I told her what I tell you.

Just as any adversity tests our strength, the feelings of being unappreciated can either kill us or make us stronger. Facing up to those feelings made Amy tougher.

In the following chapter, I'll show you how to develop a second weapon: common sense, creativity, and cleverness—the "three Cs" of intelligence. With this weapon, you'll be able to expose more cracks in the structure of your prison.

The foundation for the walls of your addiction is beginning to weaken.

Chapter 3

Common Sense, Creativity, and Cleverness

A few years ago, several medical students attended one of my Bio Energy demonstrations at their medical school. Later, three of them came to one of my sessions on stopping smoking.

During the session, one of the students, I'll call him Paul, asked if he could pose a question on a matter having nothing to do with smoking. Of course, I agreed. He was studying to become a psychiatrist, he explained, and eager to know more about my system.

"What system?" I asked.

"The system you use for understanding what makes people tick," he replied. Specifically, how did my method differ from what he and his buddies were studying in their psychology classes in medical school?

I gave him the following example: "Imagine, you see a woman, her age doesn't matter, but she's wearing a black T-shirt on a very hot day. Across the front of the shirt large gold letters are spelling out, C H A N E L.

"What can you tell about this woman?" I asked. "What do you know about her?"

One of Paul's friends raised his hand and called out, "The first thing we know is that she's very rich."

I shook my head in disagreement. A few seconds later, another student, Jesse, suggested the woman's attire means she has good taste. Again I shook my head. Paul ventured another thought, "She's probably someone who adores Chanel's designs, and everything she wears is designed by Chanel."

"No! No! No! You don't get it!" I said from my desk, aiming my remarks at the three medical students. "First of all, for sure, she's not a rich person. Most rich people won't wear anything with a designer label showing. Only people who don't have a brain will wear clothes with a designer label showing. Or possibly people who don't have money, but who want to make the world *believe* they have money will try to display it in such a primitive way. Perhaps, newly rich, very newly rich people, will wear advertising on their clothes," I finally conceded.

"Second, she's not intelligent," I continued. "Black is absolutely the worst color to wear in the heat. Why? Because it absorbs heat. Black is inappropriate for a hot, sunny day. And, we know for sure, she's not beautiful."

"Who said anything about beautiful?" Jesse called out.

"No one," I said, laughing. "I'm just telling you, we know she's not beautiful because she doesn't have taste or brains. She dresses only to impress people." As an afterthought I added, "And she's not happy."

"How in God's name do you know that?" Paul asked with a note of irritation.

"Because she cares about the opinion of others who don't care about her. That's why," I replied firmly. "And it's my belief no one will ever be happy as long as they worry about the opinions of other. This is the truth."

What I was trying to tell them was that if you want to help a person, before you do or say anything, you have to look at a person, and you have to ask, "Who *is* this person? What matters to her? What does she value?"

I could see that the three young students were less than thrilled with my nonexpert opinions. But I wanted to show them that there are many things worth learning that can't be found inside medical books.

"You can determine even more about this woman, just by looking at her," I continued. "For instance, if you were a real estate dealer, trying to sell a house to such a woman, you'd have to show her the most beautiful house in a terrible neighborhood, and then she'd buy it. Why? Because she wants to impress people in a simple and stupid way, so she will surely buy most the beautiful house in the worst neighborhood. If she had brains, she'd know it would be smarter to buy the *worst* house in the *best* neighborhood. You can always fix up a house; you can't fix up a neighborhood. It's simple. Not miraculous."

When the session ended, Paul came into my office and said, "Impressive, Mr. Shubentsov, impressive. Pretty clever. What do you call that little display we just witnessed? What branch of psychology is that?"

"Common sense and cleverness," I replied. "With a helping of creative thinking on the side. That's it, Paul, nothing fancy about it."

> "**C**ommon sense
> is not so common."

The French writer Voltaire made that observation more than two hundred years ago. I don't know what prompted these words from the great writer. What acts of human folly or self-delusion caused him to make such a declaration? I cannot be certain.

One thing I know for sure. His thoughts have stood the test of time. And today? From what I observe, although it's sad to say, late in the twentieth century, Voltaire's words are still on the mark.

At first I didn't know what a crucial role common sense and creative intelligence and cleverness would play in my treatment of addictions and cravings. In fact, when I first came to America, I didn't even know that I would become involved in the treatment of addictions at all.

But something unpredictable happened. It took me by surprise and changed the course of my life. And, perhaps, it will change yours as well.

A few years after my arrival in the United States, I was, in a sense, forced to take on the treatment of addictions in my practice. I could no longer limit my treatment to those suffering from physical pain. Why? The answer is simple.

More and more, the men and women who had traveled from all over the country to my Brookline office were plagued by problems other than the distress of acute or chronic physical pain. They were seeking my help as a healer because their lives were riddled with cravings and addictions. Cigarettes, chocolates, ice cream, alcohol, food binges of almost everything you can imagine.

I listened as one person after another told me their stories, and it seemed clear to me that many of these men and women were in as much pain as the chronically ill—only theirs was the pain of bondage.

The stories I heard saddened me. They also challenged me, both as a human being and as a healer.

I had just escaped myself from a forty-year confinement in the Soviet Union, so learning that so many *Westerners* felt confined and not in control of their own lives came as a shock to me. I had always imagined that Westerners had lives spilling over with freedom. Instead, I discovered that many Westerners felt their lives spinning out of control. I also realized the free world was experiencing an epidemic of addictions and cravings.

I quickly recognized that in order to break long-standing, stubborn addictions such as smoking and overeating, I would have to use much more than just my powers of Bio Energy. I saw that I had to learn to activate the powers that all people have within them. In other words, Bio Energy would be an important part of the treatment, but I knew it wouldn't be the *only* technique I would use.

I investigated the world of addictions, as if I were studying bacterial cells under a microscope, searching for the cause of a fatal disease. Just as a scientist analyzes the molecular structure of a suspicious cell, I attempted to analyze the forces that trigger addictions. What fuels them and nourishes them? And ultimately, what combination of forces can destroy them?

My first insight came when I took the lessons of my own experience and applied them to the problems of my American patients. I realized that just as I wasn't doomed to living out my years enslaved to the ruling dictates of Soviet ideology, my American patients should not be doomed to exist under the tyranny of their cravings and addictions.

My next insights were the ones I described in the preceding chapter. Namely, the one-two punch of public opinion and self-esteem. I've already shown you that if you slavishly follow the rules of public opinion and join the cult of self-esteem, you will be in fertile territory where addictions and cravings can flourish unmolested.

I found myself engaged in a search. My search, better described as a quest, has been to find the right key that will let you open the door to a life of new possibilities. I had one consuming idea. I wanted to create a system that would teach people how to develop willpower, how to empower people to be strong. Because that, in turn, would help to make them free.

I discovered that time and again, common-sense solutions provide a way out of the impasse. When I speak of common sense, I am talking about smarts. And to me, smarts means a special combination of common sense, cleverness, and creativity: the "three Cs" of intelligence.

I have seen this technique work like a charm on countless problems: a personal relationship in danger of being wrecked; a promising career threatened by untamed addictions; the disappointment of failed expectations amid the assault of public opinion; the pull of the cult of self-esteem.

Anyone who feels as if they're imprisoned in their own lives can be helped by common-sense solutions and by using their creative intelligence. If you feel thwarted by any sort of self-defeating behavior and wrenched by emotional problems that lurk behind all addictive behavior, you will find that common-sense solutions and creative intelligence can be lifesaving. And ultimately, life-enhancing.

After all, you've by now learned about the toughness that life inside your prison has given you. But the jails of the world are filled with plenty of tough customers. Toughness alone won't lead to freedom. It will, however, condition you to take the steps you must to be free.

This is where the "three Cs" of intelligence come in. To get out of prison, you must see doorways and escape routes, opportunities and openings where everyone else sees just barbed wire.

You have this commonsensical power within you already. You just don't know how to use it. Once you do, you'll be able to see many ways around seemingly insoluble problems. Solving these problems will take much of the heat away from the fire of your craving.

In the previous chapter, you learned that many of the messages you receive are toxic. You learned that you might reject them in favor of what you know is true.

Now it is time to take that one step farther. Now it is time to think for yourself—to take your bedrock convictions and basic knowledge and mold them into new patterns of living.

Like others, you may not be in touch with it, but once you recognize that uncommon, but precious, wellspring of common-sense solutions, extraordinary changes can occur. Like the ripples caused by a stone skipping across the water, doors begin to open. Not just the one out of the prison, but doors begin opening to other possibilities in other areas of your life.

Just as my colleagues and I in Moscow discovered that all of us possess a sixth sense called Bio Energy, so you can discover that you possess another natural reservoir of power that is equally amazing. Simply through the experience of living we acquire this gift of common sense. But too often it remains untapped, unexplored, and unexploited.

Yes, common sense is uncommon. Common sense is also perceived as many things. Old-fashioned? For sure. A cliché? Possibly. But amazing or incredible? Unlikely. Effective? Always.

I shall demonstrate that if you use common sense and creative intelligence, you will shed light on that dark small chamber where you feel imprisoned. You will be illuminating the cracks and flaws in the walls that confine you. This can help you remain free of your cravings forever. An added bonus is that you will be honing your skills for arriving at clever solutions for other difficult problems in life, not merely with addictions and cravings.

Designing Mental Karate

Let's imagine a person who is very, very afraid. The specifics don't matter. Just imagine a deeply fearful person. Now, let me ask you a question. Which is preferable for this person—to give him bodyguards or to teach him karate?

To me, the answer is simple. It's far better to teach him karate. Why? Because then he'll never have the need for bodyguards. Besides, most people can't afford to hire bodyguards, but almost everyone can afford to learn karate.

So it is with addictions. The notion of finding support with a bodyguard isn't an intelligent idea for most people. To keep people dependent on something that plays the role of a bodyguard, providing constant support, allows them to remain spoiled and reinforces their feelings of dependence. It keeps them imprisoned.

Consider my ideas a form of *mental karate,* which is my shorthand for any system that makes people strong. Only by making people less dependent do I believe they have a chance of beating their addictions *permanently.*

Discovering an Old Friend

Using common-sense techniques was similar to the experience of unexpectedly meeting an old friend after a long absence. Once I began incorporating common-sense solutions and successfully tapping the mine of creative intelligence in the people I treated, I began to attain amazing results.

Men and women who had tried every new "cure," every new system for weight loss and nicotine withdrawal, discovered they could break these self-destructive habits at last. So can you. Difficult problems, troublesome situations in life provide the fuel that keeps your addictions going, and common sense will help you sort them out.

The illustrations of the unique powers of common sense in this chapter are drawn from case histories of people I've treated. I hope you'll consider them with one thought in mind. There are life lessons within each example even if the situations don't exactly match a problem you or someone close to you is experiencing.

Common sense cannot be taught in the same way that toughness can be encouraged. I can tell you to ignore specific messages, and that's a fairly simple task. But I can't realistically expect you to suddenly start thinking creatively.

So here are some illustrations of common sense, creativity, and cleverness in action. Read them with an eye toward increasing your mental flexibility.

It's not the exact solution that matters, but rather the approach, the way of thinking, the guide to tapping into the bastion of common sense, creative intelligence, and cleverness with which each of us is endowed.

Let me tell you the story of Father Renfry.

At a smoking session, a Catholic priest appeared to be deeply depressed. As usual, I moved around the semicircle asking each person in attendance if he or she had any pain that I could treat. When I reached the place where the priest was sitting, he said, softly, "I have pain."

"Where?" I asked.

"Inside," the priest replied. "I smoke, but that's not all. I know I'm deeply depressed. But I don't want to talk about my problems."

"Can you be more specific?" I asked him. I waited, saying nothing, hoping he would continue.

"Do you really want to listen to my problem?" he asked.

"Yes," I replied.

"Do you have time?"

I said, "Yes."

His eyes were moist, and he began to speak slowly, "I'm a very old man, and my life is almost finished."

"Don't be so dramatic," I replied.

He said, "OK. I said *almost finished*. Recently I realized that on my ten fingers, I can count the number of people who came to say thank you for what I'm doing for them."

I asked him, "That's it?"

"That's not enough! You do something your whole life and nobody appreciates it? No one says thank you!" he exclaimed.

I told him, "A few seconds ago you gave me an idea, how to help you."

"How?"

"Remember, there was a day when Jesus cured ten people. They were lepers. And still he cured them. And only one person came and said, 'Thank you, Jesus.' And Jesus asked where are the other nine people? He told him, 'They're gone.'

"Think about it, Father," I continued. "They didn't even come to tell him thank you. And he saved more than their lives. He saved them from horrible suffering, too. Father, ask yourself why you, an ordinary priest, should be asking for more than God? That's not the way it's supposed to be, is it? If you decide to give, don't ask for anything back."

He became emotional and started to cry, saying, "I don't feel depressed anymore; I feel very guilty. How could I possibly forget about the story of Jesus?"

That night, he remained for the rest of the session, and at the end of the evening he shook my hand and wearily bade me good night.

Months later, he told me that the feelings of being unappreciated that had tarnished the last few years of his life were fading. Now he found himself looking forward to each of the precious days remaining in his life.

Remarkably, one minute of common sense had changed Father Renfry's life completely. Of course, it was the potent combination, common sense laced with a heavy dose of creative intelligence, that had done the trick.

If you are locked in the confines of the prison of your addictions, whether it be to smoking and, perhaps like Father Renfry, to chronic feelings of being unappreciated as well, I know the walls can seem impenetrable. The door can appear permanently sealed, and you may feel as if you truly dwell in a world that can be truly called "No Exit."

Complicating matters, as I told you in the previous chapter, there are forces all around you telling you what to do. They reinforce the illusion that you have no options but to remain chained to your addictions. But, remember, that is only an illusion.

The combination of common sense, creative intelligence, and cleverness gave me another crucial tool to break down the walls of my prison. It gave me the skills to design a perfect plan. It gave me the wisdom that showed me new paths for departure, new escape routes. It also showed me how to manipulate the Soviet system and break through the bureaucracy so that I could achieve my goal: getting myself and my family away from that hellish existence.

So I say to you, the walls that surround you are not impenetrable. There are cracks in the structure. Fortified by the inner toughness I described in the last chapter, you will begin to see that the walls of your prison are starting to crumble. And you will become that much closer to making your escape to freedom.

Earlier, I mentioned the power of these words:

> **What you're thinking, this is what your life will be.**

This thought, a perfect example of creative intelligence, was the ray of light that illuminated Father Renfry's dark world of being unappreciated.

As it did for Father Renfry, common sense combined with creativity can create a kind of cleverness that can illuminate dark corners, exposing the cracks in the walls of the prison you've allowed to confine you for too long.

For Father Renfry the power of that light had two profoundly important results. It led to his giving up smoking, which he knew was poisonous to his health. It also led to his being free of bitterness and the negative emotions that had begun to sour his entire existence.

Common sense, creativity, and cleverness are powerful weapons that can help *you* out of *your* prison. These weapons are of critical importance in handling dramatic situations like escaping from the prison of stubborn addictions. These same tools can be most useful in handling other oppressive situations as well. Less serious, perhaps, than breaking the chains of a chronic addiction, other soul-stifling problems may arise that can sap the very joy out of your life. They can strengthen the hold your addiction has on you, and they too can often be remedied by the "three Cs" of intelligence.

Let me give you an example of how the combination of common sense and creative intelligence offers an unbeatable recipe for arriving at clever solutions to a far-ranging group of problems.

In another smoking session, a man I'll call Jack Wilton told me, "It's a bad time to stop smoking. [Oh, how many times do I hear this? It's *always* a bad time to quit smoking.] I'm in a terrible marriage. In fact we're about to be divorced, but we still live in the same house and fight every day. It's hard to quit smoking at time like this."

"How long have you been married?" I asked.

"Twelve years," Jack replied, frowning. "Look, I don't hate her, but we have a miserable relationship."

I gave him the following advice. "Tonight, bring her some flowers."

"I have to bring flowers to this . . ." and then he used an impolite word to describe his wife.

Ignoring him, I continued, "Bring her more flowers the next day; in fact bring her a small bunch of flowers every day. You'll see, your life will change dramatically."

I forgot about this guy, until one afternoon he arrived at *my* office with a small bouquet of flowers. "I'm very grateful to you, Mr. Shubentsov. First of all, I stopped smoking. Second, I didn't get a divorce, and it's amazing—everything is like a honeymoon. After I left that night, I thought about what you suggested, and it sounded reasonable, worth a try. So I bought flowers, not expensive, just a few flowers. So what happened? In the morning, she made breakfast for me."

I said, "Big deal!"

"It *is* a big deal. I forgot how the hell this breakfast looked in twelve years."

So what's the point? They didn't hate each other; they had disagreements. I pushed this guy to show his old face for his wife, to show her why she loved him before, why she loved him in the first place. Then she could realize, just as he could, that they're supposed to love each other. He became the man he was when she first loved him; then she was able to act like the woman he had fallen in love with in the beginning. With that pressure gone, it became a hell of a lot easier to work on his addiction to smoking. Jack Wilton learned to think outside of the limits established for him by the terms of his marriage, and he abandoned the parameters set out by society as well. That's all the "three Cs" are. To use a business catchphrase, they represent thinking outside the box.

That's it. Simple. No genius. No miracles. Common sense. A little use of creative intelligence. And a dash of cleverness. Together, these weapons gave Jack Wilton the power to save his marriage and break his addiction to nicotine to boot.

"You're a genius!" Jack exclaimed, pumping my hand, as he prepared to head out into the night.

Genius? I don't think so. But respectful of my powers of common sense? Absolutely.

When we first met, Jack was beset by a host of worries, any one of which could have created havoc in his life. I wondered why, in fact, I *had* been able to help him through his difficult passage. If I achieved success by simply applying common sense and bringing creative intelligence to bear on his problems, why did he think that required genius? Because as I said, for sure, I know I'm no genius.

Later that evening, in the library of my home in Brookline, I was leafing through a favorite book. I happened on the words of Walter Lippmann, the distinguished American journalist. Writing about President Franklin Delano Roosevelt, Lippmann made the following observation: "The genius of a great leader is to leave behind him a situation in which common sense without the grace of genius can deal with it successfully."

I recalled other situations in which common sense had helped people like Jack—individuals who found themselves stuck in losing situations—and, after freeing them, helped transform them into winners. Still, I could understand that to the person who's life has been salvaged, it can seem like genius. I guess to someone trapped in a bad pattern, just being told that there are options sounds remarkable.

A Siberia of the Soul

Why is it that common sense, so highly valued by writers as diverse as Voltaire and Walter Lippmann—men who lived in different times and inhabited different worlds—is in such short supply? Why does it seem to have been exiled to the far reaches of our experience?

Before I realized I had the power to heal, I was an artist. And as an artist, I often think in terms of pictures. In this case, as I sat dwelling on this topic, I pictured a reservoir, brimming over, not with water, but with common sense. I ask if you'll do the same. Imagine your mind, filled to the top with common sense. Imagine too, that everyone has a similar reservoir, flowing over with this powerful human resource. Like you, others can draw on it as they make decisions, large and small, about how they will live their lives.

Now imagine the reality. This natural reservoir has become an arid basin; common sense has practically vanished. It has become like an endangered species.

When I think of common sense, it is a little like an innocent but beautiful deer, idling in a forest glen, unaware of hunters hiding in the brush.

What has made common sense and creative intelligence endangered species? To me, it seems that there are many accomplices to those hunters hiding in the brush. Many forces are at work that make common sense a fragile, endangered, but no less valuable part of the human mind.

What are some of these forces?

Rulers, for one.

The leaders of governments through the ages, be they tsars or kings or presidents, have always been fearful of the people exercising their common sense. Think about it. Do you really think these powerful world leaders are eager to face the challenge of millions of men and women using common sense? Do they really want you to use all your creative intelligence before you swallow their promises? Or cast your vote? They love popular opinion. It keeps you from thinking for yourself.

Nowhere on earth was it more necessary for political leaders to obliterate common sense than under Soviet Communism. The Communists had to bend reality, so that it would conform to their dogma, and so they had to destroy or deny common sense.

But common sense has always had its challengers as well as outright enemies. Our chronic love affair with the "new" makes us distrust common sense. Similar to any new weight-loss diet that promises you pounds vanishing "fast, easy, and forever," the promise of the hype and the intensity of your hope can make common sense seem like pale fodder next to all the glitz and glamour.

Family life, far less tight and connected than it once was, also plays a role. The fact is that when children lived near their parents and grandparents, proximity meant more than a home-cooked meal. It also meant their reservoir of common sense and creative intelligence was constantly being refilled by a steady stream of advice and stories—life lessons—all containing kernels of wisdom, the kind of wisdom that is born in common sense.

Today, like many people, you may live thousands of miles apart from your parents, let alone your grandparents. Too often the source of these "life lessons" and what passes for wisdom these days is often your old enemies, popular opinion and self-esteem, which usually proclaim what is the latest or newest to be the best or the wisest.

These days, you're more likely to get the poop about life from the Internet than from a favorite uncle or a wise old grandmother whose experiences were, to previous generations, treasure troves of value and meaning.

Filling the Reservoir of Common Sense

We know the reservoir is depleted, but that doesn't mean we can't fill it! That's part of what I do everyday. That's what I want to do for you. That's what the stories I told earlier tried to do.

In the modern world, nothing poisons common sense more than stress. How many times have I seen an otherwise vibrant, intelligent person reduced to living half a life, crippled by stress that is often completely self-imposed? In all my sessions—whether they be on smoking or overeating—the subject of stress is always up for discussion. Obviously, many people believe that stress is the number-one reason for their addictions. Whether its nicotine or chocolate, people learn through adaptation to find solace in a substance.

When stress is being discussed in my sessions, I always say, "Don't get stressed for nothing." Because to me, stress makes no sense whatsoever. Your notions of stress will always yield to a dose of common sense, creativity, or cleverness.

Consider this example. Let's say you receive bad news on a telephone call. Before you allow yourself one second to react, I want you to *stop!* Ask yourself, how long do you think the effect of this bad phone call will last? One day, one week, or one month? You can't imagine? I'll help you. Try to remember the last time you received a bad phone call. Do you still worry about that now? Of course not.

So months ago, you were bothered by something. Now you don't even think about it. So what is the reason to be worried now?

Anything that won't be important months from today isn't important at all. Promise yourself you won't let this one, new, stress-producing incident cause you one more minute of stress than it already has.

> **D**on't overpay with your emotions; you'll live longer.

Human nervous cells have no replacements. So everything that fries a brain cell hurts twice—once when it happens, and once because you're functioning with fewer brain cells. This means, if you're nervous one second, in reality in your life it's two seconds. If you're under stress for five years, the reality for the body is ten years. To me, this is obvious.

Remember Lisa? Because of her work, Lisa thought she had to deal with stress on a daily basis. Well, she wasn't dealing with it. She tried to manage it, veering from smoking to overeating to compensate for her agitation. But she was tortured by either alternative. When we first met, she had caved in to stress.

I showed her how crazy it was for her to suffer stress to make her boss rich. I also showed her how stress was shortening her life.

In time, Lisa began to make the breakthrough she needed to end her addictions. By shedding light on the nature of stress, Lisa was able to see that she didn't need to do any compensating. She no longer needed her addictions to get her through hard times. She saw how stress fed her cravings and how caught up she was in a vicious cycle. Giving her a new perspective on stress, she was able to free herself from the tyranny it had exerted over her life.

Let me tell you one more story about common sense—how useful it can be, even when you least expect it.

One evening, another fellow attending a session on overeating asked, in a slightly unpleasant tone of voice, "How do you know so much about people?"

I said, "If you look at a person, you can tell a great deal about who he is, not a hundred percent, but close."

He started to drive me crazy throughout the session. "How do you know?" he repeated somewhat angrily.

Finally I said, "Do you really want me to tell you?"

He said, "OK. Prove it."

"Let's look at you," I began. "Expensive suit, expensive leather crocodile belt, crocodile shoes, and the strap for your watch is the same color. And it's a real expensive gold watch. You have on a silk shirt without a tie and two diamond rings. This means most professions are excluded for you automatically. You're not an ordinary worker, because ordinary workers don't dress like this. They don't have enough money.

"You dress like this on purpose to show how much money you have. But it's not sophisticated to show people how much money you have. Still you dress with diamonds and gold on your body. I'm sure it's the easy way, and for some reason you want to convince people you're real wealthy, that business is great. Because you're wearing a silk shirt without a tie, this means you can afford to dress however you want. That means no one tells you what to wear; no one says it's not good to dress like this. This means you're the boss, and no one tells you how to dress, what to wear or not to wear.

"So you are the boss, and you sell something expensive."

He asked, "How do you know I sell something expensive? How do you know I'm not a doctor?"

"You're not a doctor or a lawyer. And how do I know? For the simple reason that if you dressed like this, you would frighten away all your patients or clients. The poor ones would think you're too expensive, that you would charge too much, and that you care more about making money than you do about them. In order to pay for all those diamonds and leather and silk you're wearing, they'd think your prices must be astronomical. The rich ones wouldn't trust you because they'd think you're tacky and lower class.

"Also, since it's not sophisticated to dress as you do, the work you do doesn't require a high degree of sophistication. To me this means you sell something and what you sell is expensive." I paused, and instantly I saw it. "This means you own a car dealership."

"How do you know?" he cried out.

"Common sense," I explained. "If you understand, you observe. Everything has a foundation."

Everyone laughed, including me. I'm not a mind reader, but on this day something told me that about this guy I was right. He dressed flashily, as if to advertise to the world that he was a success. And obviously, such a guy would sell something that also advertises to the world "Success!"

In fact, selling a car whether it's a Ford or a Cadillac has nothing to do with success. Success is what you feel inside, how you feel about yourself, how well you live your life. Not how well off you are.

I tell you this story to make the following point. Not only can using common sense help you in the worst of times, it can be a valuable tool to have tucked in your back pocket or stashed in your purse for those moments when all it takes is a little smarts to get you out of a jam, or solve a problem, or make a point.

Not all of our problems are so dramatic. Not all of them have the power to paralyze you, break up your marriage, or end your career. Therefore, just as I tell my patients, when you confront the hundred different life situations you experience everyday—some ordinary, others totally unexpected—before you act, *stop!* Absolutely stop and think. Is this the best way? Is this the only solution? Even if a hundred different voices proclaim a solution to be the best route, listen to your newly discovered common sense.

But all I really need to say is this:

Think for yourself.

Fortified by the inner toughness I described in an earlier chapter, and empowered by the light shed by your common sense and creative intelligence, you are beginning to see that those prison bars are not so strong. You can see the many weaknesses in the structure, the flimsiness of its walls, and the cracks in its foundation. You realize, too, that the door is not permanently sealed. Still, there is one more weapon you need to develop before you can make your escape a success.

Chapter 4

Patience and Endurance

Escaping from the Soviet Union in 1979 meant leaving the country of my birth forever. But once I made the decision to leave, I could never have imagined it would be years before the dream would become a reality.

My decision was not made rashly or impulsively. Still, each day that passed only made me more determined to leave the prison of our lives, and breathe the fresh air of freedom in the West. My wife and son, as well, became eager, hungry to make our getaway as soon as possible.

But it seemed to take forever, and we had to put our desires on hold. As it turned out, we would need patience, endless amounts of patience. Our hopes were raised and dashed and raised again. Yet each delay, each disappointment, only toughened me and strengthened my resolve. It also forced me to become more creative and clever in finding ways to beat the system that imprisoned us.

———

Turning the wish into a reality also required endurance. The endurance to bear the delays, for sure. But leaving required another kind of endurance. It meant enduring the heartache of turning my back on everything that mattered, everything that had made up the core of my family's life and my own.

But at last, the gift of freedom presented itself. Our patience and endurance had finally paid off. The news we had been waiting to hear for so long arrived. After more than two years, we were granted permission to leave the Soviet Union.

Inner toughness, common sense, and creative intelligence were essential tools that facilitated my escaping from the prison of Soviet tyranny. As you can clearly see, this one last set of weapons—patience and endurance—was also of critical importance.

So it can be for *you* as well. Fleeing from the prison of addictions and cravings is possible, if you have the right set of tools. Not only will patience and endurance help you, they can ensure the success of your escape.

After first arriving in the West, I made many discoveries that came as great surprises to me. Still, some of the differences I observed between the Soviet people and those in the free world were so dramatic that they astonish me to this very day.

For example, I am continually amazed that Westerners place no particular value on patience. Far from considering it to be of value in human behavior, quite the opposite is true. In the free world, the patient person is often seen as a plodder. A loser. A sap.

When I first realized how prevalent this attitude was, my mind was drawn immediately to pictures of my former life where, like

it or not, I was schooled in patience. So common were these images of Russians standing in lines that stretched for blocks that
they became an emblem for life in the Soviet Union, and the
source of jokes around the world.

I had flashes of other pictures as well. The bureaucratic nightmares, the endless procrastinations that were part of the simplest
piece of business. The papers, documents, seals, and stamps required for the most elementary transaction.

Did I enjoy having to exercise all this patience? Of course
not. It was mindless and largely unnecessary, but I endured it
because I had a larger plan that required patience of a different
order. This was essential patience. As the Soviets would say, this
kind of patience was absolutely necessary in order to achieve "the
greater good" for myself and my family—an escape route to
freedom.

Why is it that people who live in the free world placed no value
on patience? The answer to this question became clear as more
and more men and women arrived in my office seeking my help.
Whether they came from the United States or England, Canada,
Germany, Brazil, or Israel, their stories, though different in a
hundred particulars, shared a common theme.

Impatience was as widespread as the very addictions they
wanted me to make disappear. Impatient themselves, and forever
on a quest for immediate solutions, how *could* they value patience
or endurance? It would be like asking people whose life savings
are invested in oil wells to switch their investments and place all
their money in less risky ventures. They'd probably hold on to
their money all right, but their dreams of making a quick killing
would be lost forever.

I met individuals for whom smoking or overeating were habits of five or ten years standing, who asked, pleaded, cried, and sometimes even demanded instant cures. They wanted an end to their problems, today! Tomorrow, at the latest.

Not content to be craving cigarettes or food, these people were impatience addicts as well.

In time, I came to understand. It is true of Europeans and Americans as well as Canadians and South Americans. Because of America's unique history, it has its own reasons for making instant gratification just another inalienable right.

In the land of the American dream, the story of the shop boy rocketing to millionaire status isn't just a story. It happens, all right, but only if you hustle.

Of course. America transformed itself—the youngest nation became the strongest nation and the richest nation in record time. America wasn't just the country of *my* dreams. It was the stuff of dreams for hundreds of millions of people from every part of the world.

The settlers who built this nation and tamed its wildness came here not because they were patient. They came for the same reasons I came. They were impatient only about one thing—the lack of freedom in their lives. Why should people in the free world value patience?

I understand. I know how eager you are to seek out the *newest* solution. I know you want the latest so-called "miracle," the "sure-fire-rapid-escape-route," the "quick fix," the "magic bullet."

How could you not? The media trumpets each new miracle. Word spreads throughout the world with a speed that would have astonished us just ten years ago. If you have struggled against overeating for years, how could you not be tempted by each new miracle, especially when it promises *rapid* weight loss, pounds *melting* away, and inches disappearing *overnight?*

What I say to patients is this: imagine that you are blind. If someone told you that with thirty minutes of practice a day in several weeks you would see again, would you do it? You have been blind to this power since birth. The time has come to open your eyes.

With your eyes opened by your new powers of patience and endurance, you will be shielded from the seductive rays of the so-called miracles. You will also be immune to the downside of falling for every untried, newly minted miracle. And there is a downside, to be sure.

Allow me to be Russian for a moment. You've seen what happens when you rely on instant solutions and easy answers. Your weight yo-yos. You quit smoking . . . over and over again. And in the process you've done nothing good. All you've done is damaged your health and increased your despair.

Let me give you a perfect example from my own experience. Thousands of people come to see me, often as a last resort. Nearly every one of them tells me that they had diligently taken each new diet drug as soon as it appeared on the market. In some cases, they were so eager to take these new medications that they knew about them even before their doctors. And the result? Always, the same. The minute they went off the drugs, the weight came back. Those people were even more convinced that they were doomed to be overweight. Impatience even undermined their toughness and creative intelligence. I've heard this reasoning time and again: "I've failed to stay skinny even with the best medical science has to offer. Clearly, I'll never be as thin as everybody else." Public opinion comes sneaking back.

"I guess there is something wrong with me. Nothing works, I can't see any way to change, so I might as well indulge." If that's not an absence of cleverness, common sense, and creativity, I don't know what is.

I cannot stress enough how essential it is to develop your patience and endurance. Without it, you will undo your toughness and abandon the "three Cs" of intelligence.

In 1996, overweight patients and their physicians around the world thought they had finally discovered the ultimate answer. A diet medication, known as Phen-Fen or Redux, was approved and marketed as the diet drug to end all diet drugs. Originally designed to be prescribed for seriously or grossly overweight people, Phen-Fen was also prescribed for millions of people who were overweight, but by no means seriously obese.

Hailed as the greatest miracle drug for weight loss, Phen-Fen became an overnight sensation. Advertisements and endorsements trumpeting its wondrous effectiveness appeared everywhere. Public opinion, shifting focus from some other newly discovered miracle, took up the cry.

The media pounded out the message. People were losing tons of weight. Quickly. Effortlessly. As the pounds disappeared, people said they were filled with self-esteem. Each lost pound only increased the patients' love for their doctors. Doctors were proud of their patients. Everybody was happy. And because diet miracles make pots of money, the pharmaceutical company was happy, too. There were no side effects. No problems.

But there *was* a problem. As Phen-Fen swept the country, I began to hear from people who had suffered serious problems after taking the new miracle drug. Several had grim stories to report. As it turned out, these individual horror stories had the makings of a crisis that would rock the medical world. The crisis created living nightmares for both overweight patients and their doctors.

Gaining back the lost pounds after stopping the drug wasn't the only problem. A far more serious problem would emerge. Because Phen-Fen was so new, no one really knew its long-term implications or what side effects might occur after a person took it, as thousands did, for months at a time.

At first, word began to leak that some people were developing disturbing side effects. Then the news became alarming. Grave reports of critical illnesses caused by these drugs were growing in number. Not ordinary side effects like a little headache or mild nausea. We're talking about major illnesses affecting people's hearts and the functioning of their lungs.

More alarming reports appeared, and still more, until September 16, 1997. After serious heart-valve complications were diagnosed in disturbing numbers of people who took the drug, the drug company withdrew Phen-Fen from the market.

The army of public opinion had to shift gears once again. It turned out that Phen-Fen might be as effective at destroying vital organs of the body as it was in making unwanted pounds disappear.

Three months after the drug was removed from the market, the FDA urged *everyone,* anyone who *ever* took the drug, even for a week or less, to consult their doctors and be examined for possible damage to their hearts or lungs.

The strangest part of all this is what I witnessed on television the night the drug was recalled and in the newspapers for weeks later. One person after another appeared in utter despair, complaining about what the loss of this drug would mean to their lives. Devastation is the word that best describes their emotions.

Phen-Fen *had* to be available, they exclaimed. It had been their salvation. They had lost hundreds of pounds with it. Why would anyone take away anything so marvelous? How would they ever be able to function? How would they ever feel good about themselves again? How would they ever maintain their self-esteem? It was as if they had found the holy grail, the precious secret of true happiness, and it had been snatched from their grasp. Why was the world standing by and letting this terrible thing happen?

I found this incredible. Remember, they were saying this *despite* the known dangers, *despite* the risks. Rather than breathing a sigh of relief that this dangerous drug was being labeled for what it was—dangerous—people around the world wept on television, declaring that they felt victimized and deprived.

At the same time as this drama was unfolding in the media, I was seeing hundreds of patients who were equally desperate about the loss of Phen-Fen. Along with the excess baggage of unwanted weight and their food cravings, they brought to my office another craving—their cravings for miracles, their need for instant gratification. And magic bullets.

But I have no miracles up my sleeve. I can help them, just as I can help you. But to remain permanently free of your addiction, to make your escape a success, I tell you what I tell my patients. You will have to give up the search for miracles and your vulnerability to the latest fad. Instead, you must replace that addiction with the weapon of patience and endurance.

If you are a prisoner attempting to escape from prison, to be absolutely certain that you'll remain free, you must destroy the prison. Only then can you never be recaptured. If you act impulsively, grasping at every easy solution, believe that every "revolutionary" plan is fail-safe or the "true path" to freedom, you are buying into another one of the myths of the army of public opinion. If you act rashly, without considering the consequences, you can be killed or taken back to prison.

You must remember that freedom isn't a relative term. It's not something you can qualify. You can't be a little bit free.

Exercising patience and endurance can help you become totally free. Let me give you another example of the trouble you can get into when you indulge your craving for instant fixes and follow easy escape routes to freedom.

Consider the nicotine patch and nicotine gum. To me, they offer only a qualified kind of freedom. They will make you feel a little bit free of your craving. To me this means you are still locked behind the prison bars of your addiction.

My admonition against using nicotine patches or gum is this. If they were so effective, or at least as effective as their advertisers claim they are, wouldn't most insurance companies have paid for them when they were available only by prescription?

Imagine that you're the president of a large health insurance company. Ask yourself, if you're the owner, which is better financially for your company, which makes better business sense: to reimburse people for the patch or the gum if it will prevent smoking-related illness or to reimburse them for the illness? To pay, for example, for a coronary bypass or rehabilitation therapy following a stroke or for the prolonged treatment for cancer— surgery, radiation, prolonged hospital stays, chemotherapy? Or would you rather pay a few bucks for the patch?

If these nicotine replacements or alternative nicotine delivery systems are so effective, why didn't most insurance companies reimburse people for the cost of these cigarette substitutes in the days of prescription-only availability?

Isn't it simple business sense? If insurance companies believed these substitutes worked, if they had evidence that they effectively reduced the astronomical costs of cardiac or cancer care, don't you think these companies would have paid for them?

Stop a moment and think about it. Even if the insurance companies were willing to pay for some method of maintaining your nicotine habit, do you really want to replace smoking with another nicotine delivery system filling your body with the stuff?

It's a scientific fact that all traces of nicotine are gone from your body in seventy-two hours. I repeat, seventy-two hours. That's it. Of course, the psychological effects can go on for months. I will discuss this in more detail in the chapter on stopping smoking.

But isn't it worth enduring the seventy-two hours of physical nicotine withdrawal to be really free? I believe nicotine substitutes, the gums and patches, are designed for those who don't have the endurance to bear seventy-two hours of withdrawal. For people who don't want to use their common sense and recognize that they have just shifted their addiction from one form of nicotine to another.

Substitutes keep you locked in the prison of nicotine addiction.

If you want to be free of cigarettes, you can't be a *little bit free.*

Another Day, Another Miracle

Just read a newspaper or turn on the evening TV news. Another day, another miracle. A never-ending roster of miracles appears, and those that draw the most attention are the ones that promise to keep you either eternally young or eternally thin. They are so tempting, these promises. I'd like to find such a miracle myself.

It's difficult to resist the promise of a miracle, particularly when it comes to weight loss. Particularly when it promises *rapid* weight loss, *instant* weight loss. Particularly when you've been battling the problem for as long as you can remember.

Each miracle diet has its moment in the sun, when the glare of public opinion dazzles the promise of perpetual thinness before the eyes of the chronic dieter.

If you are a chronic dieter, you know the feeling. Exhausted by the search, frustrated by the constant ups and downs in your battle with the scale, your spirits are sagging from being let down by too many promises. Word of a new miracle can be like an elixir. Sad to say, it merely ignites the same old cycle of raised hopes and dashed expectations. It plays havoc with your toughness and dampens your desire for creative solutions.

The people I see in my office already feel as if they've crossed the country in search of a miracle. They've done the Scarsdale Diet and the Beverly Hills Diet and spent some time in The Zone. They tried the diet that tells you what to eat based on your blood type. They followed the one that said not to eat steak and potatoes at the same meal, and diligently followed another that had them keeping vats of cabbage soup simmering on their stoves, day and night. The only diet they haven't tried is the one that tells you what to eat based on your horoscope. Probably because it hasn't been invented yet.

They've tried no-fat and high-fat. High-carbohydrate and low-carbohydrate, high-protein drinks and low-protein powders. At one time, each of these diets was dangled before the public's eyes as the miracle du jour.

But when it comes to weight loss, there are no miracles. Instead, behind the scenes, in the factories where miracles are manufactured, there are cynical minds at work.

The following is a favorite illustration I use in my sessions to show how diet miracles can be manufactured and merchandised.

Many of the diets that you've read about recently recommend eating seven times a day. I know that's a popular idea, and I also know why it is particularly adored by people in the business of selling diets.

Let's imagine, for the sake of argument, that you and I own a diet company. You're the president. I'm the marketing executive.

You ask me, "How can we sell more diets? If we don't sell as many diets as possible, we're not going to be successful, and we'll have to go out of business. Should we keep selling these three-meal-a-day diets?"

I'm a clever marketing manager, so I would answer, "Let's sell them seven meals a day. In fact, if we tell them to eat seven times a day, they will buy, I'm sure of it."

"Why is that?" you might ask.

"Because they *already* eat seven times a day," I would reply.

So you see, this notion of eating seven times a day is pure business, nothing else.

Remember my former patient Brian? Overweight and chain-smoking when we first met, later he returned to tell me he had been able to escape from both addictions. He, too, had tried every fad diet, every appetite suppressant, each new nicotine withdrawal system. He had tried everything except patience and endurance.

By tuning out the voices clamoring for his attention, and the sales pitches for fads and diets clamoring for his dollars, he made another choice. He realized the unwanted pounds wouldn't, *couldn't* drop off his body overnight.

So he consciously made the choice to follow a course that required *patience*. Patiently, he chose to eat sensibly and followed my recommendations for weight loss. Patiently, he managed to find the time to exercise every day. He had to dig deep within himself and find the endurance to keep the program up until the scale told him his patience had paid off.

Also, he gave up the patches and the gum and *endured* the seventy-two hours of physical withdrawal from nicotine, all the while following the tips I gave him to keep him away from cigarettes.

Brian broke out of the prison of his addictions. According to his last letter, he is still free and it's been more than four years since he first came to my office.

Many of the people I see don't want to hear about patience. They want me to make everything easy.

In time, I came to see that it's the Western way. You have to *love* to do something. Because loving it will make it simple. The wish is for everything to be simple. Easy. Emotional. Miraculous.

Love doesn't play a role in my system. In the next chapter I'll show you why. But determination does. If you've got the determination and you add to that the values I've described, you're on the way to destroying your prison forever.

It's a three-step system that works. In the following pages I'll show you how to put all the weapons together. I'll add them to the arsenal of proven tips and techniques—the ammunition for your weapons.

1) Inner toughness, so you can resign from the cult of self-esteem and ignore the dictates of public opinion

2) Your powers of common sense, creativity, and cleverness
3) Patience and endurance

Imagine having all these weapons working for you as a synchronized, well-oiled machine—a machine that will knock down the walls of your prison forever.

Ready? I'll show you how.

Chapter 5

Destroying Your Own Prison

Everyone who visits my office has the same goal. The specifics may differ, but each of them really wants to become free of cravings. Just as I know you want to be free of yours, or you wouldn't be reading this book.

Even those who come to my office for a Bio Energy treatment must participate in their own cure. You who are reading this book have more responsibility. But you are not merely a passive empty vessel. You must be engaged. I asked if you are ready. Now I ask if you are *determined.*

> Determined to break free
> Determined to remain free
> Determined to say good-bye to the fads and the search
>   for miracles
> Determined to develop inner toughness

Determined to resign from the cult of self-esteem

Determined to ignore the shifting winds of public opinion

Determined to hone your creativity, to dip into your untapped reservoir of common sense

Determined to be patient and enduring

I know, I'm asking a lot of you. A lot of determination. I ask this of you because I know I'm presenting you with a powerful set of tools. It took *all* of these weapons to make my own family's escape a success. When I hear from former patients, however different their individual problems were, it is always this combination of weapons that helped them destroy the prisons that had enslaved them.

I want you to *use* all these weapons at your disposal. But let me tell you what I mean when I say "use." I know a woman who is eighty-eight, and I'm sure she thinks she uses a hearing aid. The truth is, after all of her friends badgered her for months and told her she really needed it, she agreed to use one. I say, agreed, but we still have to repeat everything we say to her at the top of our lungs. Why? Because, even after she spent the money and bought one, she so dislikes the idea that she leaves the hearing aid in her top drawer. So again, I say, you have the weapons. Don't let them sit in some compartment in your mind. Use them!

What Does Love Have to Do with It?

I promised you I'd say something about love and the role it plays in escaping from cravings. Let me explain. When I lived in Moscow, I spent a great deal of time working with members of

the medical profession. So when I compare the differences between Soviet doctors and doctors in the West, my observations
come from firsthand knowledge. I observed them not only from
the point of view of a patient, but as someone who worked *with*
them as well.

When I came to the West, I discovered that the attitudes and
assumptions of doctors in the free world were very different from
those in the Soviet Union. Now I see that each of us is shaped by
the social and political forces pulsing through our different cul-
tures. How could we not be different?

So it didn't surprise me when I observed firsthand that the
expectations and needs of patients in the West were also mark-
edly different from those I observed in Moscow. Oddly enough,
the first and most profound difference involves the concept of
"love."

I was surprised by the doctors. Of all my impressions, the most
striking one was how much they wanted to be loved. By com-
parison, Soviet doctors didn't give a damn. I'm not sure anyone
else in the USSR did either.

Listening to the stories of thousands of men and women struggling to lose weight, and to the stories of doctors as well, I came
to a conclusion: love appears to play an essential role in any transaction between a patient and a doctor. That is to say, doctors in
the West believe they will be more loved if they promise x pounds
lost in x days on this diet or that. Indeed, this is true of any doctor attempting to treat the problem of overeating—or who's
treating a patient for any addiction for that matter.

Let me offer an illustration. Consider for a moment a common
occurrence that takes place between Western doctors and their patients. Let's say a woman, I'll call Julia, is deeply disturbed by her

inability to control her weight. She goes to Dr. Jones whose examination confirms her fears. Not only is she seriously overweight, but Dr. Jones warns Julia that the excess pounds are endangering her health.

It's my opinion that Dr. Jones, similar to many doctors, wants Julia to become "his" patient—a frequent, if not chronic, visitor. Julia's much more likely to become that loyal patient if he can win her love. I'm not talking about romantic or lustful love, I'm talking about a pure, 100% affection—the esteem everyone in the West seems to be searching for.

One way for Dr. Jones to win that love is to agree totally with Julia's explanations for *why* she overeats. As Julia explains *her* reasons and tells him why she always feels hungry, Dr. Jones listens compassionately. Nothing unusual about this? Not yet.

Like many patients, as Julia gives her account, she may cite unlikely reasons for overeating. Unlikely to me, that is. She may claim that it is the misery of her early life, the lack of love from a distant mother, for example, that is the root of the problem. If Dr. Jones shares her belief that the primary cause for her overeating lies in her childhood, he's on the way to winning her affections and her respect.

Even if Julia is fifty-five, the doctor can be persuaded that it's the emotional pains of the past childhood that are causing the excess pounds of the present. If Dr. Jones accepts as gospel any one of a hundred reasons Julia may offer for indulging in her cravings for food, he's likely to win the love of his patient. He may not be really persuaded by her rationale, but Dr. Jones understands that Julia cannot control her weight. He doesn't want to alienate her by saying something she doesn't want to hear. So, he agrees that there is nothing she can do about her weight. He is on the road toward medicalizing her problem. Julia gets what she wants: a deflection of blame. She has sold Dr. Jones on her conviction. "It's not my fault I'm overweight. There's nothing I can do about it." Dr. Jones is going to give her an easy out. The pounds are going to melt away.

Dr. Jones, in turn, gets a new patient, the satisfaction that he's helped someone, the side effect of return visits, and the ego boost from being godlike.

The newly created bond between them will make Julia a loyal and chronic patient. Leaving his office, she can tell herself and her world of friends and family how much she *loves* her doctor.

Dr. Jones is not alone. Regrettably, in thousands of other doctors' offices throughout the world, the same transaction is reenacted daily. The patients serve up the notion that a loveless childhood or an unfulfilled life expectation is the reason for their being overweight. They offer every possible explanation and always conclude it's beyond their control. Time and again this happens. And time and again, doctor and patient agree. Whether it's actually uttered, or accepted as an unstated fact of life, the conclusion is the same.

Food is so tied up with love and the patient's emotions that she can't help herself. Food and love (or the lack thereof) have become one and the same.

If Julia insists on accepting this notion, it means she will remain locked in the prison of her cravings. If she clings to the "food is love" argument, she will not have the determination to draw on all the tools in these pages.

If Dr. Jones accepts Julia's explanation, he's not being at all malicious or deceptive. He's merely doing what Western social interactions and medical training expect and frequently demand. But he's not lying to or misleading his patient; he honestly believes that by bowing to his patients' rationalization, he can provide the best care.

Dr. Jones maps out a weight-loss program for Julia. Still eager to please his patient and give her what she wants, he assures Julia he will give her a diet and exercise program that is highly effective. Now Julia's other craving takes over—the addiction to instant gratification. She asks, "Isn't there an easier way?"

I have described what can happen when doctors and patients alike share the desire to find the magic bullet and administer the quick fix and—poof!—together, they make a miracle. The results of the Phen-Fen *miracle* will adversely affect the lives of some of its victims for years to come.

There's another side of the love equation. For people in the West, emotion seems to be a strong motivator. Loving or not loving something is an excuse for indulging in self-defeating behavior. Love is part of our emotional life, and it's a part we don't have total control over. So when our desire for food or aversion to exercise is raised to that same emotional pitch, we have yet one more excuse. "It's love," we think. "It's beyond my control."

An attractive woman named Beth, who could be much more attractive minus about fifty pounds, opened one of my Saturday evening overeating sessions to announce, "But I love cheese!"

"You don't love cheese," I told Beth. "You love your husband, but you *like* cheese."

Another voice from a woman on the other side of the room piped up, "That answer may work for Beth. But what if you don't have a husband?"

Laughing along with the other members in the group, I added, "I repeat, husband or no husband, you like cheese. Love isn't the issue here; it only seems that way."

I was trying to make a serious point in a lighthearted way. As I mentioned earlier, it frequently amazes me to hear how often the word "love" is used by people struggling to overcome their various cravings.

Besides, as I explained to Beth, loving cheese is not in her genetic program.

Nor is it in yours.

Your body is born with a dramatic desire to eat, but it's a *general* desire, not a specific one. You were born with a basic desire to eat, yes, but not with a basic desire to eat nuts, chocolates, or ice cream.

Similar to Beth, the people who come to my office ask me not only to make everything easy but also ask, "Can you make me *love* exercise?" In fact, 90% of the people who come to me to lose weight have asked me that question.

I always insist, "Exercise is different; it's not a husband or boyfriend. Exercise has nothing to do with love. It's not even connected."

In time, I came to see that it's the Western way. Unlike in Russia, people in the West have to *love* to do exercise. But I say, you don't have to love it, you have to *do* it. Willpower is not genetic; willpower is training. There is a very big difference.

For many people, if it's not love, it's hate. They ask, "Can you make me hate chocolate?"

"Love the treadmill?" "Hate ice cream?" "Love salads?" "Hate sweets?" The specifics may differ, but the essential wish is the same. For everything to be simple. Easy. What could be simpler than love or hate? Not a matter of personal choice.

Let me share with you the story of a most unusual patient. His problems were unique, and it took all the weapons I have described in these pages—inner toughness, common sense and creativity, patience and endurance, and determination—all working in combination, to get him out of the prison of his problems.

This same combination can be a winning strategy for you as well. It can help you get out of the worst kind of problems as well—be they personal or professional. Or, as it was in this man's case, trouble both in his home life and in his business. And big trouble it was.

Three years ago, at one of my stopping-smoking sessions, a guy showed up looking just awful, as if he were a refugee from a junkyard. His clothes disheveled, his face unshaven and darkened by a spirit of utter despair.

When I met him in the reception room before the session began, I learned from Anna, my secretary, that his name was Will Riley. I asked her if he had just wandered into the office, but she assured me he had made his appointment six months before. At the outset of the session, I moved slowly around the semicircle pausing before each person, using Bio Energy on a young woman's sore elbow, caused by a skiing accident, and on an elderly man's bad ankle, the result of a fall. Finally, I found myself standing in front of Will Riley.

I watched as he shifted slightly in his chair. His eyes, heavy lidded and half-closed, opened slowly and met mine as he said quietly, "As you can see, I'm upset, and I feel terrible."

Although I had the distinct impression that in his case it wouldn't be a sore ankle or a painful elbow that was causing the problem, I asked routinely, "Where is your pain?"

"All my life is pain," was his terse reply.

"Can I help?" I inquired.

"Nobody can help me," he replied glumly. After a few seconds, he began to sketch out the recent details of his life that had led to his air of defeat.

"I'll tell you," he began, choosing his words carefully. "I used to sell insurance, and I was doing quite well. I met a wonderful woman, we married, and bought a great house. Now, for some reason, I'm not successful. Everything's changed. My life is a mess, we have a new baby, but no money, and my wife and I don't stop fighting. Even my parents are angry at me!"

Allowing time for this litany of misfortune to sink in, he paused a few moments before adding, "I'm very depressed—the mortgage on the house . . . everything's gone to hell. How am I going to stop smoking? And if I'm not smoking, I'm eating everything in sight. I don't even know what I'm doing here."

With that, he shook his head and buried his face in his hands. Before tackling the issue of his smoking, I decided to take another approach and asked him, rather matter-of-factly, "Who are the most difficult people to sell insurance to?"

Without looking up, he replied, "Yuppies."

"Why is that?" I asked.

"Because they're young, they're strong, and they're healthy," the answer came swiftly. "They have good education, good position, good money, good health, good prospects. What the hell do they need insurance for?"

Depressed as he was, I decided Will was still a man who knew his business. Although I knew practically nothing about the insurance business, I had the glimmer of an idea about how to help him and thought I'd give it a try.

"All right," I said, "I'll give you advice on how to sell insurance to all yuppies in the United States."

Looking up, his eyes were riveted on me. Even though he was studying me as if I were certifiably crazy, at least, I thought, I had his attention. His expression said it all: "What did a Russian healer know about the care and feeding and selling of insurance to yuppies?"

I raced on, "The next time you go to sell insurance to a yuppie, I have a few suggestions. Be sure to tell him that you know, in fact you absolutely understand, that he has no need to buy insurance. Tell him the reasons are obvious."

Will interrupted, "You *are* crazy!"

"Listen to me," I continued. "Never lie to your customer; tell him the truth. Then go on and tell him, 'I know you're young, you're strong, you're healthy, and you don't need life insurance, what for?'

"Pause a few seconds, and then address your yuppie customer this way. Ask him, 'But your good education that gave you this position? This cost your father a lot of money, didn't it?'

"Let this sink in, then continue, saying something like this, 'Let's say, your father has a lot of money and he really doesn't need anything from you. *Financially.* But what does any father need? *Appreciation.*

"So many of you Americans feel unappreciated. So, use that to *help* you for a change. Make the self-esteem cult work for you. Tell him to say to his father he's going to take out a one-million-dollar insurance policy on his life, for his father. Tell him to say to his father, 'I travel a lot. This is in case something happens, this is for you. It's a small reminder of how much I esteem you.' And the father will be deeply touched.

"Then you can tell Mr. Yuppie that you can promise it won't cost him a lot precisely because he is so young and healthy."

"I think you're nuts," Will Riley said, albeit with a sly smile.

I'd heard that before, so I answered Will this way, "I'm telling you, if you'll do what I say, it will dramatically affect your business."

"How can you be so sure?" Will's eyes had finally opened; he was hooked.

"Do you like to fish?" I asked.

"I do, so what's the big deal?"

"No big deal. Do you sometimes use a big green fly attached to the reel to attract the fish?"

"Of course I do."

"Do you ever want to eat that big green fly that you're using as bait?"

"Are you kidding? Me eat that?"

I told him, "When you want to fish, you use bait; you have to use what the fish likes, not what you like."

So what's the point? Three years later, Will returned to my office and he was ecstatic, brimming with good health, smiling, beaming. Sitting in front of my desk, the words poured out of him, "I'm doubly grateful."

I asked him, "Why double?"

"First of all, I quit smoking, and nobody could believe it," he replied. "Second, right now, I made one hundred thirty-two thousand dollars after taxes last year. All yuppies' money! Now, can you tell me how to sell insurance to other people?"

"I take it things have improved," I observed, noting with pleasure the transformation of this man who, a few years before, had been in this very chair, on the verge of emotional as well as financial bankruptcy.

"Improved? Life is a dream!" he exclaimed. "I've paid all my debts. My family is great; we're about to have another baby. How did you do it? Was it the Bio Energy?"

I shook my head. I told Will that while Bio Energy can accomplish many things, and doubtlessly had helped him break his addiction to nicotine, I seriously doubted that it was the key to the dramatic turnabout in his life. After all, coming up with inspirational business tips isn't my specialty. As for advice on how to make a killing selling life insurance to disinterested yuppies? That isn't something I had studied in Moscow or America.

"It's common sense. It's also intelligence, but a particular kind of intelligence. The kind that calls for creativity, for cleverness," I told him. "It's the kind of cleverness that tells you it's not what you sell that's important. What's important and what you have to understand is the mentality of the people you're selling to."

"Incredible!" he said.

"I don't think so," I said. "All I did was show you how to use powers you already have. As far as everyone else is concerned, I think you can figure out how to sell insurance to them without my help."

Days after my last meeting with him, I was still thinking about the gains Will had made, not just in selling insurance, but in every corner of his life. The more I thought about it, the more clearly I came to understand. Will was able to combine all the weapons I've discussed in the preceding pages and make them work in concert.

Think about it.

He had to develop inner toughness to withstand the dramatic downturn in his career.

His tough inner core had another job as well. It had to be strong enough to throw off the messages from the apostles of his former religion. He had to be able to say, "My problem isn't low self-esteem from a failing business. It's that I eat too much and smoke too much."

To do this, he had to immunize himself against the easy excuses and blandishments of public opinion. He had to ignore the insulting messages that society peddles, messages that say, "You can't quit, you're weak, and your cravings aren't your fault. They're the fault of your mother or your father, your job, the economy, or the world."

To work his way out of a financial hole, he had to be creative and clever and use his common sense.

His creativity made public opinion work *for* him. For instance, public opinion says yuppies are as concerned about the fate of their aging parents as they are about the future of their school-age children. Public opinion also says they have dollars to spend. Will just had to find a clever and creative way to reach them.

He had to have the patience and endurance to keep to his plan and to turn his failing marriage around.

Above all, he had to be determined to do all this.

And he had to do all this and not necessarily *love* every moment of the process. But in this process, Will saved his marriage and his business.

You must do this, too. Mobilize all the weapons now at your disposal and make them work for you. See these messages of public opinion and the lure of low self-esteem as insults to your intelligence and to your common sense. Let them make you angry, as they should.

Those excuses should offend you for other reasons. They allow you to keep smoking until you've received a Ph.D. in self-esteem.

Don't take the easy way out. Because it's a false exit, a trapdoor. Be patient. Have endurance. Be clever. Make a plan. Be cunning. Tune out anything that diverts you from that path. Then you won't be hunted down and killed like a fugitive or recaptured and put behind even stronger bars. Then there will be no prison that can hold you. You will have destroyed it bit by bit as you made your escape to freedom.

Now you know the weapons you will need to free yourself from the prison of your cravings.

In the following chapter, I'll tell you about another unusual power that you possess—Bio Energy. It alone can't erase your cravings—it took me almost thirty years of practice to get to that point. But it can make the journey to a craving-free life much easier. It can also enhance the toughness you will soon develop, the creativity that's about to burst forth, and the patience that has been lying dormant. All you have to do is tap it.

Once you tame a power you didn't know you harbored, anything will seem possible—even solving the insoluble.

Chapter 6

The Sixth Sense:
Principles of Bio Energy

Imagine a large but otherwise unimpressive building in the center of Moscow. It is the middle of the 1970s. The Iron Curtain still separates East and West. Words such as perestroika and glasnost are not yet part of the world's vocabulary.

Imagine, too, that within the walls of this Moscow building, an odd conglomeration of people are hard at work. Can you imagine hundreds of men and women giving up their free time to work strictly as volunteers, receiving no money in return? At a time when every ruble was so precious, when every Soviet family's dream was to harbor enough money to have an apartment of their own?

Try to imagine as well that these volunteers are trying to harness a form of human energy that is both invisible and immeasurable. Does it sound a little crazy? Yet, that is what they are doing. Why? They do this day after day, because they believe this mysterious energy has the power to heal, the power to reduce pain, even eliminate pain entirely. They call it Bio Energy.

Finally, imagine that it's twenty years later. A Russian émigré who managed to escape from the oppression of Soviet Communism is using this same Bio Energy to help tens of thousands of people from all over the world. Not only is he freeing people from physical pain—after more than thirty years of study and research, he is using this same extraordinary energy to help people escape from the prison of their addictions and cravings.

So Who the Hell Am I to Tell You All These Things?

It may seem that I'm a Russian blowhard imposing my beliefs on a bunch of suffering people in the free world. But I come to my knowledge and my profession quite honestly. And quite remarkably. So that you don't think I'm completely crazy, let me tell you how I became a healer.

It was an ordinary spring afternoon. I was sitting in the office of a publisher for whom I worked as a freelance commercial artist, chatting with another artist who happened to be in the office that day. After we talked for a few minutes, he said the strangest thing in the most matter-of-fact way, "You know, you have a very strong energy field; I can feel it."

I must have looked baffled, because I had not the slightest notion of what he was talking about. Grinning, as if my reaction were not unusual, he went on to explain, "Most people have this energy to some degree, but in them it's never tapped. Yours is already very well developed. I'm involved in some experiments in this area. If you'll give me a call, I can't promise you anything specific, but I can promise you an interesting life."

He handed me a card with an address scribbled on the back. I placed the card in my wallet, yet for several weeks I thought nothing more about our conversation. But his words continued to haunt me. I would put the idea out of my mind for days, but it would return. My natural skepticism was losing to my sense of curiosity. In the end, my curiosity was triumphant.

Late one afternoon, after I had dropped off a batch of illustrations at the publisher's, I went to the address he had written on the card. I recognized that it was a well-known building in Moscow, one I had passed many times before—Popov's Laboratory.

I didn't know exactly what to expect. But I know I anticipated something that resembled a scientific laboratory, or at least what I imagined a scientific laboratory to look like—a world of test tubes and computers, beakers of brightly colored chemicals arrayed on shelves, and scientists bent over microscopes studying slides, and a smell, an aroma that was a distillate of all the chemicals and test tubes, the vapors of scientific inquiry.

But it was nothing like that. I remember my first impression vividly. Everything looked funny, odd. People seemed to be working or talking in small rooms. They didn't look very serious, not like people involved in scientific research *should* look.

It was, in truth, a baffling scene. All these people working in teams in different rooms. No computers, no microscopes, no test tubes. Instead, men and women studying plants and flowers. Instead of beakers filled with chemicals, objects made of wood, stone, wool, and plastic were arrayed on tables. I thought it all looked very unprofessional, but when I met the researchers, I was surprised to discover all of them had good educations. In fact, many of them had Ph.Ds. But what were they doing there?

That night, I told my wife it was a bit disappointing. "It's all very odd," I explained to Viera, "and I don't have time to spend with crazy people."

My wife said, "Why not? It's interesting, and it seems like serious people are involved. They can't all be crazy—not with so many Ph.D.s."

After a few days, I convinced myself to make another visit to the laboratory, and something interesting happened. It didn't appear to have been orchestrated, but rather seemed to be quite spontaneous. After being introduced to me, everyone I met told me I had unusual, unbelievable amounts of Bio Energy. It was as if they were speaking a foreign language, because they couldn't explain exactly what it was.

What did I possess that was so unusual? Generally, you *know* if you have a talent for something—to sing, or to be an artist as I was, for example. It's strange to learn that you have a special ability or talent, one you haven't already discovered for yourself. So, when people try to describe this supposedly marvelous talent, and you can't grasp for yourself what they're talking about, that can be confusing, maddening, and in a way, I suppose, seductive.

After I returned to the laboratory a third time, I told Viera she was right. "They seem completely normal," I reported.

My wife, a scientist herself, was intrigued, and so, I admit, was I. It was curiosity that brought me back again and again. In time I learned that for most of the people engaged in these experiments, money was not the motivation. Like myself, most of these researchers—scientists and nonscientists alike—had other jobs and were volunteering at this laboratory.

Perhaps it sounds strange—hundreds of people working in a laboratory for no pay, experimenting with something that couldn't be seen and frankly seemed a bit occult. But there were many inducements, emotional bonuses, for those of us who volunteered to work with Bio Energy.

Because of Soviet Communism's ban on religious expression, the lure of being engaged in something that was related, however vaguely, to a belief system had a charm of its own. To be part of something that was spiritual—even a *tiny* bit spiritual—if only because it was inexplicable, drew eager researchers and, I admit, skeptics like me.

In short, who could pass up the chance to indulge in something that was connected with the mystical, the unknown, and therefore prohibited? Not me. And not the hundreds of others who found their way to the laboratory every day.

In most countries in the world, if I were to open a laboratory, but I couldn't offer any money, who would work for me? Scientists or nonscientists? Of course, no one would come. But in the Soviet Union, even without money, everyone including scientists came, happily. It was probably one of the few things people in Moscow were allowed to do without coercion.

Why? Apart from the aura of being involved in something slightly forbidden, it had the added attraction of igniting our curiosity, and, quite simply, it was fun.

For others—some unhappy men and women who didn't feel successful, who wanted to improve their role in life—working in the laboratory offered them the rare opportunity to feel like *somebody*. Even though my own work wasn't dreary, and I took pleasure in being an artist, I must confess it was thrilling to be part of this research on Bio Energy. It was interesting, yes, but we also worked at it because the results were more and more encouraging. How could we not be crazy about it?

The most thrilling moment for me occurred when I discovered that I had the ability to heal, that my own Bio Energy could end a person's suffering.

It came unexpectedly. Similar to the happenstance way I first learned about this strange force, my discovery that these powers were real and actually could help people came without warning.

It began undramatically, as just another day in the laboratory. In the afternoon, a well-known professor was making a tour, observing our work. As he made his way through the laboratory, he told us that he frequently suffered from migraine headaches. In fact, he admitted, he was having a crushing headache at that very moment.

Later, one of the researchers tried placing her hands over his head, but her attempt at healing failed. Nothing happened; the professor's pain was unrelenting.

For weeks I had seen some evidence, in much smaller ways of course, that I did indeed have some special powers in my hands. But I was apprehensive; it seemed immodest to even think I could offer him relief.

Somewhere I found the courage and asked if I could try to help him. When he agreed, I stood behind him and placed my hands over his head. Within a few minutes, the professor looked at me, startled. For the first time in days, he told me, grasping my hand in gratitude, his pain had begun to disappear. A few minutes later, he shook his head in disbelief and exclaimed, "I have no pain, no pain at all!"

As for me? I was completely shocked. I knew this was a serious man; he was not someone who would pretend he was being healed to gain attention or celebrity. He was already famous because of his own accomplishments.

The professor returned weeks later; his pain had not returned. As for me, nothing could prepare me for the total transformation that would become my fate.

Not every day was so dramatic. We continued to work on fundamentals and made very few efforts to do more work on humans. I was beginning to understand the experiments that at first had seemed so bizarre. They were designed to answer crucial questions. Could this thing called Bio Energy be harnessed? Could it be used for military purposes? Could it be used to help people? Could it help in healing? Could it work when other medical treatment failed?

Months later, when I was asked to work as a healer in several Moscow hospitals, I would leave Popov's Laboratory and find the answers to some of these questions in a new setting.

By now, you can easily imagine for yourself that working in Popov's Laboratory was an exhilarating time. But it had its moments of confusion and self-doubt. All my life, I'd studied and worked at being an artist. It had been my calling, my career, and, what's more, I had achieved a notable degree of success in that career. But now, with each passing day, people were seeing me through a different lens. They believed, and I came to agree, that I really had this power or gift or talent.

As you can also see, at that point I still didn't know what to call it or where it would lead or what it meant. I still didn't know if it was something only I possessed or, as I know now, a talent that all of us can awaken. I was beginning to get glimpses of this new self. In other words, Yefim, the artist, was beginning to coexist with this new person—Yefim the healer.

Coexist, for sure. But was the success I had achieved with the professor just an isolated occurrence? Would I ever be able to achieve similar results again? I didn't have a clue.

On that extraordinary afternoon, all I knew was that I, along with the other researchers with whom I worked, had witnessed something we had scarcely allowed ourselves to dream of: the same Bio Energy that intrigued so many of us had the capacity to do far more than anyone anticipated. Amazingly but still inexplicably, Bio Energy could reduce human suffering!

But what else could it do? With this new power, I was fearful that we could possibly do harm as well as heal. So for months we avoided doing any further tests with humans until we had dug deeper—exploring, searching, seeking to understand what was really going on.

Back to the Drawing Boards

My original impression of the laboratory was that it wasn't exactly scientific. I remember thinking to myself that if you do something every single day, sooner or later you're bound to achieve a positive result. But that doesn't necessarily prove anything. I thought we had to go back to the beginning. We had to become more scientifically based—that is, we had to get results 100% of the time before we could consider our tests a success.

We knew that we were still dealing with the unknown. So with renewed respect for the potential powers of Bio Energy, we returned to the laboratory's initial studies.

For instance, working with seeds, we returned to the preliminary tests. Dividing them up into two batches, we tried to discover if plants would grow faster and stronger if they received doses of Bio Energy from our hands. When it worked, as it invariably did, we were heartened.

Hour after hour, day after day, we performed the same experiments, again and again. Could we feel from a leaf if something was wrong with the tree? How did leaves feel if they were healthy? How did they feel if they were diseased?

We moved on to flowers. If we cut flowers and put them in water, did they last longer if we placed our hands over them? The answer to all these questions was inevitably, habitually, yes, almost 100% yes.

In our work with growing plants and flowers, we never had negative results. This "life energy," as we began to call it, made everything better.

The nagging question was *why*. Why did this happen? What did some of us possess in our hands that could make plants grow stronger and faster? Did everyone have it? Could you develop it? And, most baffling, why couldn't we measure this energy?

Most of us weren't scientists, but we knew enough about scientific methods to know that in order to understand this mysterious power, in order to be taken seriously, it was crucial for us to find a way to measure, record, in some way capture—be it with numbers or counters, photographs or tapes, computers or seismographs—this still mysterious force.

In an attempt to solve these questions, every conceivable kind of instrument was brought to our laboratory. Fanning out all over the city of Moscow, we searched for machines that might be capable of measuring this energy.

But the results were utterly maddening. It was like trying to take a picture of a current of wind passing through the air. We could witness the transformation that came from this energy in our hands, but we could not measure it. Compasses, thermometers, Geiger counters, nuclear scanners—even with the most sensitive machines, nothing. No needles moved; no numbers changed; no lights blinked; no graphs jumped.

It was simply impossible to record the changes that were apparent to the naked eye. The only proof we had for the existence of Bio Energy were the observations we could see for ourselves each day. We told each other that if and when we had the opportunity to work with a human patient again, surely then we'd find the means to measure our work.

Mysticism, Miracle Workers, or Magic?

In my hours away from the laboratory, I became a student. I studied everything I could find, trying to learn about others who had also experimented with new forms of energy. How did they grapple with the intriguing but stubbornly unyielding questions that I faced every day in Popov's Laboratory?

I discovered that Franz Mesmer, for example, who in the eighteenth century had coined the notion of animal magnetism, discovered quite accidentally that it wasn't only the magnets that were achieving the remarkable results. He was able to achieve similar reactions without them. The key to his work seemed to be something he possessed within *him* . . . in his head and his hands.

I was unschooled in the subject. I was amazed to discover in my reading that the existence of another form of energy—a healing energy that could alleviate suffering—had been around for generations.

From my reading, I realized I was only following a path that many others had traveled for ages, probably since the beginning of time. At other times and in other civilizations, this energy has been called many things. The Ancient Chinese called it Chi or Vital Energy. The Ancient Hindus knew it as Prana. And in the eighteenth century, Mesmer labeled the force Animal Magnetism. Later, Wilhelm Reich called it Orgonne Energy. Some Soviet scientists call it Bioplasmic Energy, and contemporary Czech scientists know it as Psychotronic Energy. But for us, it became Bio Energy.

I was beginning to see myself as part of a tradition. I was like these other dedicated individuals, who found their imaginations utterly captured by a mystery. Wherever and whenever the concept of a mysterious form of human energy has emerged, in Europe or Asia, in ancient or modern times, it has been understood as a life force that binds all of us together.

Each century and each civilization has also had its doubters and skeptics and nonbelievers. Some brave souls who attempted to tap into this reservoir of life energy so that it could be used in the art of healing have been variously scorned as witches or misfits, religious zealots or psychotics, and often complete charlatans.

Fortunately, as you'll soon understand, this was never a problem for us. Ours was not the usual experience, and we never had to face the kinds of obstacles encountered by past generations of researchers.

Take the attitude of most mainstream religions, for example. Religious leaders have rarely offered warm welcomes to those who dared to delve into what had always been considered the unknowable, the domain of God. Yet, performing miracles of healing is not only acceptable to most religious traditions, it's often, in fact, a crucial test, a proof of saintliness.

For Jesus, healing was seen as dramatic proof of his divine origins, and therefore he became a figure sanctioned, anointed to be the object of worship. The attitude changes when healing is performed by persons outside the church. Then, rather than providing proof of saintliness, it became grounds for damnation. This condemnation often led to imprisonment, inquisitions, and witch-hunts, if not worse fates.

Happily, for me and my associates in the Soviet Union, none of these dire consequences loomed as potential threats; they were never even an issue. While the Soviet leaders would make death, exile, and imprisonment the tragic fate of millions of its own citizens, and the gulags were crowded with those who in some way had challenged Soviet authority, Bio Energy research was never seen as a threat to the established order.

There were two reasons for this. The first is simple. Atheism was part of the air we breathed in Moscow. For us, there were no Sunday sermons laced with flaming indignation decrying our intrusions into the great unknown. In fact, our own skepticism about all things mystical had the ironic effect of both complicating and enriching our work. On the one hand, we'd think, "If Bio Energy isn't mystical, then what the hell is it?"

We couldn't rely on God as the genesis of these powers because, according to the dictates of Soviet Communism, God didn't exist for us. Without God-given talents, we believed this energy was somehow connected with humans, maybe with all animals.

In a real sense, something positive actually did come out of the rigid, godless Soviet party line. It liberated us, so our minds were free and exploding with questions and ideas. How could we explore this energy? How could we do this? Could it be transferred from one individual to another? Was it inherited? Could it be taught? Could it be used to cure illness? Alleviate pain? Not once or twice, but reliably, almost every time?

The second reason came one day as I was sipping my morning mug of coffee. I had an unsettling realization: the military and the KGB had to be deeply involved in our experiments. They had the resources to pay for our large building that was an expensive piece of real estate in the center of Moscow.

Are We Brainwashing Ourselves?

After our successful experiments with plants and trees, we were ready to move on. Before we began the next phase—working with animals, which seemed a natural development—we stepped back. We had to pause and assess what we knew. I began asking myself, "Are the results we're achieving merely a projection of our wish to succeed? Are we simply brainwashing ourselves?"

To answer these nagging doubts, I developed a series of experiments on how to sensitize our hands, so we could feel things more acutely. I introduced them to my colleagues in the laboratory. In time, we had mastered these exercises, and in test after test we were able to prove that these exercises I'd devised could activate our hands. We could indeed sense the difference in plastic or metal, colors, materials, and fabrics and, without touching them, identify them.

We realized that even if you had unusual amounts of Bio Energy, you had to be trained. Everyday we tried to make it work— metal, plastic, stone, marble—until, eventually, we could actually feel the differences in colors and shapes and fabrics without touching them, just by passing our hands through the air above them. Remember, I was an artist, accustomed to working with colors. But to be able to identify colors without looking at them or touching them was astonishing. These results were becoming consistently good and, at times, I would say even shockingly good.

In time I would teach these same exercises to physicians both in the Soviet Union and the West. In the next chapter, I'll show you how to perform a refined version of these exercises, designed to enhance your toughness, creativity, and endurance. You can activate the Bio Energy in your own hands. This new power will be invaluable in giving you added confidence. An invaluable asset in your battle against cravings and addictions.

From Plants to Animals

The time had come for us to proceed—to see if Bio Energy could be used to help animals who were in pain or diseased. As we entered this level of testing, we learned that in order to heal living things, we had to transform energy from ourselves to this other being. To do this, we knew, required utter concentration. We also knew that we had to protect ourselves. For example, I had to be sure my energy was flowing toward the animal, but I had to be equally sure I wasn't taking away anything vital from the animal itself.

Although it was almost thirty years ago, I vividly remember our first experience with an animal. One of the guys who worked with us brought a friend's dog to the laboratory. None of us knew what the problem was; all we knew was the dog didn't seem well, wasn't eating, wasn't his usual vigorous self.

He was a brown and white basset hound, friendly, and betraying only moments of being dispirited, indications that he was in pain. Without touching him, I could feel he had some sort of problem with his rear right leg. After I placed my hands over the dog, it was apparent in a few minutes he was able to walk with no signs of distress. When his delighted but puzzled owner returned and took the dog out of the laboratory, several of my colleagues and I lingered, savoring the moment.

Bio Energy worked. For sure. It had cured the professor's headache. It worked on plants and seeds, and now, it had worked on this dog. I looked at my hands, and if I could have spoken to them, I suppose I would have said, "I don't know where the future will take us. But I know we can't stop now."

With each new experiment, the suspicion that we had brainwashed ourselves faded more and more into the background. It was Bio Energy, not our eagerness or hopes for success that had led to our successful treatments.

Much later, after we began the serious research of using Bio Energy to treat humans, we questioned why animals appeared to react to Bio Energy better and faster than humans. In time, we found the answer. More than humans, animals are accustomed to reacting naturally. Animals have to survive and adapt more by instinct, respond more spontaneously to changes in their environment than human beings. Animals don't have beliefs and skepticism. No preconceived notions were holding them back from feeling better.

Conversely, animals don't experience the placebo effect, so the positive results we achieved when they recovered and when their pain was gone were due to only one thing, the power of Bio Energy.

An Artist in the Hospital

I was so busy that I was oblivious to the fact that news of our work was beginning to spread throughout the Soviet medical establishment. When our work became known to several interested medical directors of hospitals, we were offered the opportunity to treat people in a medical setting.

Doctors from the cardiology department of a leading Moscow hospital made the proposal that we try to do our work in their facility. It was exciting but unsettling. It was one thing to volunteer in a laboratory, but the idea of working in a hospital?

At first, it was an informal agreement. From time to time we would perform Bio Energy treatments on patients who were experiencing pain. The doctors were always standing by, observing the results. After further experimentation, we made agreements with other hospitals, and with each invitation, the agreement would become more concrete, more formal.

Looking back, because even today it seems so odd, I must remind you that all of us had other jobs—biologists, artists, even professional military people who had been told they had high amounts of Bio Energy. No one received money; we simply shared our information and shared our knowledge.

Viewing this through a non-Soviet prism, I can understand that all of this must sound very strange. But there was no objection from the medical staff. Medical doctors were allowed, even encouraged, by the chiefs of hospitals to try something new, as long as it wasn't dangerous. Besides, the doctors were always present, carefully observing my work. In a sense, they were using me as an instrument.

In time, that informal invitation was transformed into an official agreement between the hospital and those of us performing the healing. Although we now had official status, the medical personnel were always in control. Our first experiments were in sports injury and cardiology. The results were impressive. For example, people who had undergone surgery not only healed more rapidly when treated with Bio Energy, but they did so with less pain and required far less medication.

Once we began working in a hospital setting, the atmosphere

changed perceptibly. I felt a growing internal pressure; my own sense of responsibility grew astronomically. Imagine what a challenge this was! To be working with people, trying to end their pain.

The pressures also increased because of the conditions set down by the hospital. The doctors exerted their own kind of pressure. For many hospitalized patients, time itself would make people better. They told us that in order to determine if our healing energy really worked, our cures had to be rapid.

So the pressure was on: heal and do it fast!

Later, after I had developed a reputation as a healer, I was invited to work in the Pediatric Hospital in Moscow. Unlike previous invitations, this was an official offer. Not only would I wear white robes like the physicians, for the first time I would receive payment for my work as a healer.

Incredible! Only months before I was a simple commercial illustrator. Suddenly, I was wearing white robes, teaching physicians the art of Bio Energy and healing their patients.

Of course there were parameters in which I worked. I only treated those children who were suffering from illnesses where medication wasn't necessary. Never were any of the patients' lives at risk. In addition to working with patients, I also was asked to instruct the other doctors in the techniques of healing through Bio Energy.

It was an enormous leap to go from Popov's Laboratory to the Pediatric Hospital. Just as it was an enormous leap to go from trying to feel the specific energy of the color red, to standing side by side, next to a physician, trying to feel the source of a young child's pain.

To hold your hands over planted seeds to make them grow

faster and stronger is not the same as holding your hands over an elderly woman's head in an attempt to relieve her crippling migraine. To accept the latter is a challenge that requires a daunting sense of responsibility.

It's a leap I made and a challenge I faced, as did several of the other researchers. From the vantage point of many years, and from a non-Soviet perspective, one might properly ask, "How did Soviet doctors feel about all this?"

You may be wondering, "Why did Bio Energy develop in the Soviet Union? Why not Canada or Europe or the United States, where most other medical advances are made?"

It's a natural question, and people ask me about this all the time. The notion of nonmedical practitioners working as healers in a hospital setting is something that can scarcely be imagined by people in the West. Especially in the Soviet Union. In a country so regimented, so controlled, how could this kind of unconventional research be pursued in a hospital setting by people with no medical training?

Medicine Minus the Money: A Different Breed of Doctors

To really understand why Bio Energy developed in the Soviet Union in the 1970s, you only have to look at the different attitudes of doctors in the West and those I worked with in Moscow.

First, there was no resistance from the medical profession because Soviet doctors didn't view us as competition. We threatened neither their prestige nor their bank accounts. Since medical care was free, Soviet doctors made the same amount of money if they had one patient or one hundred patients. They didn't benefit by having repeat patients, just as they didn't benefit by having crowded waiting rooms. So they were happy to have us pursuing our experiments, however strange or offbeat these experiments appeared to be.

Soviet doctors didn't seem to mind discovering that something they hadn't learned in medical school could offer their patients even a tiny bit of help. Why? Because of *zero* competition. If a doctor saw a hundred patients a day or only one, the money was the same.

The second reason also has its roots in a factor peculiar to a Soviet Communist society. In my entire life in the Soviet Union—forty years—I didn't know one doctor who was sued by his patients. They didn't even have malpractice insurance!

This doesn't mean Soviet doctors weren't punished for their mistakes. They were, but it was by the government. For example, if a Soviet doctor killed a person, he could be put in jail, maybe even executed. But if he injured a patient, he wouldn't pay money to the patient or his family. Money wasn't punishment. With money taken out of the medical transaction on every level, nontraditional therapies could thrive. And anyway, if there was one thing we were certain of, it was that Bio Energy was perfectly safe.

Imagine how Bio Energy would be viewed in America or most countries in Europe. The Western medical establishment has scoffed at alternative treatment for years. Acupuncture and nutritional remedies—to name just two examples of unconventional care—despite some progress in acceptance by the medical establishment, still face tough going in numerous hospitals and virtual nonrecognition by many health insurers as well.

In this context, can you picture a former commercial artist being allowed to use Bio Energy to heal patients in a Western hospital? When I am involved with any medical people in the West, it has often been my experience that the medical doctor often thinks of himself as the first person after God. So to mix his name with some crazy Mad Russian isn't something he's eager to pursue. His reputation doesn't need it.

Soviet doctors didn't care about their reputations, at least not in that sense. Because Soviet doctors didn't have such an exalted view of themselves as Western doctors do, they allowed us, even *invited* us, to perform our method of healing in their hospitals. Not because they were more humane or caring than Western doctors, but simply because the more chronic patients they had, the more miserable their own lives became.

Why? Because when Russian doctors gathered for their monthly meeting, they were asked by officials, who had the most chronic patients. And if it was you, you looked damn stupid because you didn't know how to help people. Soviet doctors were willing to learn with pleasure *anything* that would possibly help them heal people faster.

To me, it is an irony. In the free world, people in fact have not actually been so free—not when it comes to medical care or being free to choose alternative care in a hospital. But we are beginning to witness a change. An old adage may explain this changing atmosphere best: "No doctor wants to be the first to try a new cure, nor does he want to be the last." Some of these restrictions are loosening, but healing through Bio Energy remains a thorny issue in many countries throughout the world.

Whenever I had a moment, I continued to study all the books I could find that would tell me more about this mysterious energy I was using every day. I devoured everything in print on healing energy. In one book, written early in the twentieth century, I happened on a study that struck me as amazing.

According to this study, it seems that in an ant colony, as long as the queen ant remains alive, all the other ants belong to that society. But only as long as she remains alive. In fact, if they attempt to go to another ant colony, they will be killed immediately. How do the ants in the new colony recognize the intruders? No one knows. However, once the queen in their own colony dies, these same ants would not be considered intruders in a new colony and would be accepted by them. In turn, that new colony's queen puts her mark or energy on them. Once again, they are somehow encoded with this invisible bond; if they tried to enter yet another colony, they would be killed. That is, until this new queen dies. It is an invisible bond.

I came to understand that although we cannot measure Bio Energy, time and again we can see these results; we have signs that it exists. The best analogy, I think, is that of a signal from a radio station. If there is a storm and the radio station transmitter falls to the ground and is destroyed, the radio signals persist in the atmosphere forever. As far as we know, they travel into space endlessly. So it is with Bio Energy.

How Bio Energy Works

First, let me tell you what it isn't. Bio Energy isn't electric; it's not magnetic; as I've indicated, we don't yet have an instrument with which we can measure it. That doesn't mean it will be impossible to measure someday. Years ago, we couldn't measure gravity or electromagnetism, but it's possible to measure them today. Five hundred years ago, nobody knew about nuclear energy; now we know how to measure it.

We do have an indirect way of measuring the results of Bio Energy techniques. We can measure the results before and after a cardiogram, before and after healing, before and after taking someone's blood pressure. So while we cannot measure the energy itself, we can measure the result of treatment through Bio Energy.

Earlier I told you an ancient fable. Remember the angel and the old man? The angel knows this old man could be the greatest warrior the world has ever known. Just as that old man sitting in the marketplace doesn't know he has the power, you haven't known till now that you too have the power of Bio Energy.

But you do.

When I lived in Moscow, I discovered an old book about acupuncture from the days of Imperial Russia. In this book I found the answer to a question that had been tugging at my mind. An ancient healer, quoted in this book, observed that the fingers are the exit for the body's energy—this means they are doorways through which energy can travel.

Through my Bio Energy exercises, I can help people find a way to open their doors so that they can feel their own energy, activate their own energy. My hands will be like keys to open the doors and get in touch with this remarkable energy.

Just as I showed my colleagues in the laboratory how to activate their hands and instructed doctors in Bio Energy techniques in hospitals both in Moscow and the free world, I will show you how to open your hands and make them more sensitive, more active. You'll be able to feel things you've never felt before.

In my office, I use it as part of my method for treating addiction as well as pain. To me, Bio Energy is like the discovery of a sixth sense. It's a sense you can acquire; it is teachable, learnable, and, once you master it, you can use it in different ways.

You can relieve pains in your own body as well as in those closest to you—your friends, your family. And with this new power awakened in you, you'll see the strength you already have—the strength to quit smoking, control your weight, and stop your cravings.

Please remember, Bio Energy is not a substitute for medical treatment. You must always consult your doctor when you are feeling unwell.

You won't begin as a master, you'll begin at the bottom of the staircase. And step by step, level by level, after you practice these exercises, you'll reach the point where you can tap into this vital life source.

What Bio Energy Can Do for You

Bio Energy cannot erase your cravings; it took me three decades of practice to get to that point. But when you tame a power you never knew you harbored, anything will seem possible—even solving the insoluble. And combining it with the other lessons in this book can cure your cravings once and for all.

So now—on to the energy within.

Chapter 7

Discovering Your Sixth Sense

As my work with Bio Energy became known to members of the medical profession, both in Moscow and Boston, I was asked to instruct doctors on how to develop their own powers of Bio Energy. On numerous occasions, I have demonstrated a series of exercises that describe in a concise and clear manner how to discover this untapped resource—this healing form of energy.

In this chapter, I will show you what I've shown the doctors— how to develop your own Bio Energy. The descriptions of the techniques and exercises are simple and easy to follow. I explain, step by step, how you can go through the different phases of developing this new force. The drawings accompanying each exercise illustrate precisely the position your hands should be in for each exercise.

It is my experience that these exercises work for everyone, without exception. However, each person's experience may be different. You will begin with simple exercises to sensitize your hands. In fact, in less than three minutes after doing the first exercise, your hands will feel active in a way they never felt before. With more practice, you'll be able to sense things you never sensed before. When you have finally mastered all the exercises, I will show you in the final exercise how to transform energy from your body that *may* be helpful in healing someone else's pain.

Let me emphasize, when I say you will be able to help heal someone else's pain, I am not saying that using Bio Energy in any way replaces consulting a medically trained physician or following the course of treatment or the medication recommended by such a professional. I am only saying that using Bio Energy can be an additional method of speeding up the healing process and of alleviating the pain of minor injuries or simple headaches, for example.

But Bio Energy should never be used instead of consulting a doctor or following his or her advice.

When you begin this program, I recommend that each week you learn one new exercise. Always begin your exercise session with the exercises you've learned in previous weeks. This is not time consuming, as you will realize once you begin the program of exercises listed below.

Now, let's tap your Bio Energy.

Exercise 1: Activating Your Hands

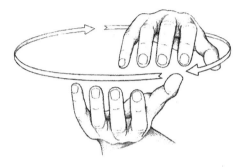

Begin with your left hand open, with your fingers spread apart. Imagine that you are holding a ball the size of a cantaloupe in your hand. Put your right hand in the same loose position. Float it above your left hand, with a distance of about two inches between your palms.

Rotate your right hand around the fingers of your left hand in a clockwise motion for about thirty seconds. Maintain the form of your hands, but try not to make them tight or tense. After thirty seconds, reverse hands, and move your left hand over your right hand again in a clockwise motion for thirty seconds. You will feel your hands becoming activated.

It's important in the beginning to keep your eyes open as you learn each new exercise. The reason for this will become clear in the following sections when I describe the more advanced signal exercises.

Exercise 2: The Exit

Remember, before you begin this exercise, repeat the first exercise you learned the previous week.

The second exercise is designed to open the exits of energy that are located at the end of your fingers. Place your right hand in the same position as it was in the first exercise, keeping it open and loose. Extending your left pinkie, move your left hand over your right hand and make small clockwise circles over the pinkie on your right hand. Do this for thirty seconds.

Wipe the fingers of your left hand clean of any residual energy by brushing your left thumb against their pads.

Return your left hand to the same position as before, and rotate the extended pinkie of your left hand, clockwise, around the ring finger of your right hand, again for thirty seconds. Again, cleanse your fingers. Continue doing this for all the fingers of your right hand. Then, repeat the foregoing exercise, with your left ring finger making the rotations. Continue this exercise, with each finger of your left hand making the circuit of rotation over every finger of your right hand.

Now, turn your hands over, holding them in the same relative position. This time, beginning with your right pinkie, make the clockwise motion over the pinkie of your left hand. Continue doing this so that each finger of your right hand makes the clockwise motion over every finger of the left hand. Do exactly as you did before until you feel the sensation of energy being activated in your hands.

Do this twice a day for one week. I recommend doing the first repetition of these exercises the first thing in the morning.

Exercise 3: The Cage

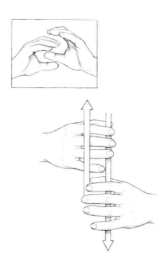

Begin by activating your hands and practicing Exercise 2 for several minutes. Remember to keep your eyes open.

With your fingers slightly spread, form your hands into the shape of a U with your thumbs on one side and your fingers on the other. Place your right thumb into the center of the U formed by your left hand and, with a slow up-and-down motion, move your hands past each other. Your hands should be about nine inches in front of you; the flat of your hand must face your sternum.

Then reverse the exercise. Switch hands and repeat the same motion.

Slide the thumb of your left hand through the cage created by the other hand for one minute. Move your hands up and down, gently. Do this at least three times a day for about one minute per hand.

Exercise 4: The Expanding Balloon

Begin, as you always do, by activating your hands. Then perform all the exercises you've been practicing in the previous weeks.

Place your hands six inches before you, with your palms perpendicular to your face. Your fingers should be slightly spread as if they are holding a small water balloon. With a slow, pulsing motion, imagine that you are feeling the pressure of the water balloon. Slowly move your arms apart while keeping up the pulsing motion. It should feel as though the water balloon is expanding with every pulse. As the balloon gets bigger and bigger, concentrate on feeling the pressure it exerts on your hands. The expanding balloon will soon force your arms completely open.

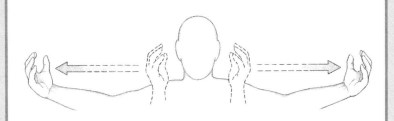

Now that the balloon feels as if it is at its largest point and your hands are the farthest apart, move the fingers on your right hand a bit as if you were playing the piano. You will feel pressure in the corresponding fingers of your left hand. Do the same with the left hand, moving your fingers as if you were playing the piano, and you will feel the same cascade of movement in the other hand.

The next step is to compress the water balloon and to imagine feeling it return to its smaller size. As you feel it getting smaller and smaller, move your hands closer and closer together until they return to their original position.

You might feel more sensitivity in your left hand. Don't be surprised. This is true of the majority of people.

Perform this exercise three times a day.

Week Five

Sensitized Hands

Spend the fifth week practicing all the exercises you've learned up to this point. Your hands are now sensitive, activated in a way they've never been before. In other words, your hands are now more open. You're now ready to learn how to feel the first signals that your sixth sense will be sending you.

Remember: you must regularly perform all the exercises you have already learned.

Exercise 5: Learning the Signals

Now that your hands are open and sensitive, the following exercises are designed to show you how to understand the signals that come from different objects.

Begin, as you always do, by activating your hands. Place your left hand over the border of your desk or a table. Slowly pass your hand over the edge of the table or the desk. You'll feel a warmth coming from the object that is absent when you pass your hand over the empty space. The edge will be a clear boundary between the warm air and the cold air.

Remember to keep your eyes open. This is essential.

Why?

It is simple. Understand, you are beginning to create an encyclopedia of signals in your brain. To do this, you must associate what you're feeling with what you are seeing. Soon, with practice, you'll be able to detect these same signals without using your eyes. But for now, keep your eyes open.

This is the first time in your life you will be able to feel something without touching it. Enjoy the moment. You can't touch it; you can't smell it. You can't hear it or taste it. It's your sixth sense. And you are using it for the first time in your life. Congratulations.

Do this exercise three times a day for one week until you are confident that you are detecting the different signals.

Exercise 6: Colors

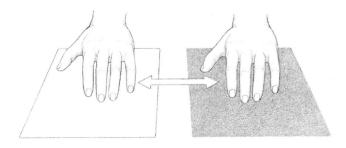

Begin, as always, by activating your hands, performing all the exercises you've learned up to this point.

Place two pieces of paper—one white, one black—side by side. Place your left hand over the piece of black paper. Concentrate. Focus on the paper with your eyes. Feel the energy coming from the paper. Then, glide your hand over to the piece of white paper. Focus and feel the difference in the signal.

Remember to keep your eyes open so they can see what your hands are registering. You must look directly at the object as you detect the signals with your newly sensitized hands.

Soon, you'll recognize that the black paper will project a signal that is warmer than the one coming from the white piece of paper.

Do this exercise three times a day. Continue doing it until you are confident you are detecting the dramatically different signals coming from the two different colors.

Once you are confident that you can distinguish between black and white, it's time to try your hand, so to speak, on other colors.

With several different colors of construction paper, perform the same exercise as above.

Remember that you are creating a dictionary of signals in your brain—a dictionary of signals of how different colors feel.

At the end of a week or so, after you have performed these exercises every day, you can give yourself an examination to see if you've learned the signals of each different color. Ask someone to place the pieces of colored paper in a random order. To test, pass your hand over the paper with your eyes closed. Try to determine the color of a piece of paper from its signal alone.

If you're 80% correct, that's great!

You should repeat this library-building exercise with objects of different materials. Instead of colors, use wood, plastic, metal, or whatever. Learn to sense the characteristic energy of each substance.

Now, apply your newfound sensitivity to the forms of objects. Feel the distinct signals coming from a briefcase, a coffee cup, a telephone. Ask yourself, "What is the shape of this object? Where are its edges?" Draw on your database to determine its composition and color. Mentally catalog the sensations these more complicated objects produce. Concentrate on which aspect of the object you are feeling for. Trying to identify shape, color, and composition at the same moment will only confuse you.

I cannot emphasize this enough: Do not close your eyes. I know from instructing physicians in hospital settings that the temptation will be to close them, but remember that to educate yourself, you must see with your eyes what your hands are sensing. Close your eyes only when you want to test yourself. You are making a library of sensations, and you'll need as much information as you can get to assign a meaning to each signal. After all, a card catalog is absolutely useless without the books to back it up!

Soon, you'll find yourself confidently detecting the signals from different materials and forms, opening up the database that is in your mind.

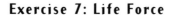

Exercise 7: Life Force

You are now ready to try to detect the difference between animate and inanimate objects. For example, try to feel the difference in energy when you pass your hand over freshly cut flowers and ones that are a week old.

Learn how the energy of a live plant feels when compared with that of a dead one. (Most people seem to have a lot of these.) Concentrate and feel the distinct energy of each state.

Now, it's time to sense the difference a healthy plant feels as opposed to one that has been injured. Don't worry. You don't have to cut down a tree to do this. Simply tear the leaf of a plant in half. As you concentrate on its energy, you should be able to discern the unique feel of a damaged life force. If you just bend the branch of a plant or tree, you will be able to sense how that energy feels as well.

It is essential to recognize the sensation of a damaged life force, especially when you begin to think about relieving pain.

Now try to feel the unique radiations produced by an animal. Just hold your hand over your pet. The feelings you receive will be dramatically different than anything you've detected before.

Practice this whenever possible. Catalog how the different parts of the animal feel through your Bio Energy.

There are additional signals you can add to your dictionary of sensations. Moving things, for example. Try this exercise:

Go to the sink, and turn on the water. Circle your relaxed hand, with your fingers spread, around the stream flowing from the faucet, and concentrate on the unique feeling that movement has.

You must always tell yourself what you are looking to feel. Do you want to identify colors or forms? Animate or inanimate objects? Movement? Damage? You have a big database of Bio Energy sensations, but you must tell your brain into what category to place each sensation. This way, when you want to identify something, you will know where to search.

Some advanced practitioners of Bio Energy (myself included) have learned how to apply this same sensitivity to the unique energy given off by a body in pain, by a damaged joint, by an inflammation. With this information—this diagnostic tool—an experienced Bio Energy healer can determine the source of a person's health problems. By using his own Bio Energy, a healer can reduce the signals of pain or inflammation in another person. In order to do that, the healer must project energy out of his own body, through—where else?—his hands.

You can learn to project your energy as well. You will, I promise, be overwhelmed by the power you possess. But let me say right now that you should never use the techniques we're about to discuss for anything other than exploration. Any medical condition, any aches, pains, or distress should be attended to by your health care provider. These exercises are meant to demonstrate the power that resides in you. They augment your toughness, creativity, and endurance, and the power they engender makes the stranglehold of cravings easily broken.

I haven't assigned a week to the following exercise because you should only attempt it when you feel you are ready. I cannot tell you how long you should spend on the exercise discussed earlier. You should just explore. This is the beginning, after all, of a lifelong enterprise.

You'll know when you are ready to begin radiating your Bio Energy. It will happen when you realize that your Bio Energy has become second nature, when, almost unknowingly, power seems to flow from your fingertips. Then you are ready.

This is the moment when your Bio Energy becomes active rather than passive. This is when you learn to access your healing Bio Energy.

Exercise 8: Radiating Energy

Activate your hands, as always.

Sitting up straight, rest your forearms on the top of a table or a desk. Move your right hand to the center of your chest, and hold it a few inches in front of your sternum.

This is your center chakra, and it is the point from which you should visualize all of your Bio Energy flowing.

With your eyes open and following the progress of your movements, slowly move your hand up to the base of your neck, over to your left shoulder, and down the top of your left arm. Your hand should remain a few inches above the surface of your body at all times. As you follow this movement with your eyes, imagine that a pulse of energy from your chakra is traveling up to your shoulder, down your arms, and out through your fingers. Visualize this pulse of energy, and push it out through your fingertips.

Practice this until you can actually feel the energy flowing along its path. I promise you; it won't take long.

Once you are certain that you can make the energy flow smoothly, push it along its journey without your hand. Using your eyes alone, visualize the pulse passing from your chakra to your fingertips. Before long, you should be able to do this without much effort.

Now, reverse hands. Using the same steps as before, move Bio Energy from your center chakra to your right fingertips. Do not be surprised if the sensations of power are weaker on this side of your body. That's quite common.

Here comes the fun part. With both hands resting on the table or desktop, push the energy out through the fingertips of *both* hands. Concentrate. Visualize the twin channels of energy you have opened crackling with a strong force. Envision that power streaming out of the gates in your fingers. You are now radiating Bio Energy. With practice, you will find it easier and easier to project your energy. You won't have to concentrate nearly as hard or sit absolutely still.

You can also experiment with healing minor aches and pains with your Bio Energy.

However, under no circumstances should Bio Energy take the place of a visit to or advice from a trained physician.

I must stress that you view Bio Energy healing as an exploration of your own powers alone. Any troubling pain or condition should be treated by a medical practitioner.

If you have a friend or a loved one with a simple ache, you can tap into your Bio Energy and try to relieve the pain. Without touching the person, hold your hands over or wrap your hands around the spot that hurts. Try to project your energy around the area of the body where you feel the signal for distress. The pain should melt away underneath the power of your energy.

Bio Energy is an essential part of the treatment I offer to those who come to my office in Brookline. You can master the same exercises we used in Moscow, those I still use today both in my practice and when I instruct physicians.

Bio Energy and Your Cravings

Do not expect to erase your own cravings with your newly awakened Bio Energy. As I've said before, it's taken me thirty years of practice to be able to erase cravings with my Bio Energy. It's a treatment I can only perform in person. Unfortunately, I cannot do it through these pages.

However, I promise you that if you embrace the new perspective we've talked about and add to that your Bio Energy, *you will leave your cravings behind.* Your smoking, your overeating, and your other compulsions will be a thing of the past. You will not only escape from your prison, but you will also demolish it.

Enhancing the Three Virtues with Bio Energy

This newfound power now coursing through your system is a remarkable thing. Before these exercises, you could not sense color, shape, life, or pain with just your hands. An entirely new sense— a sixth sense—has awakened within you.

There are many things you can do now that were once impossible. There is a world of perception that is no longer opaque to you.

Your personal power has been greatly augmented. Isn't it logical then that other things you thought impossible might just be doable? Doesn't it seem much more likely that your cravings will yield to your determination? After all, you couldn't "see" objects with your hands before either. You couldn't radiate energy through your fingertips before!

Your way of interacting with the world has changed forever.

What was inconceivable before—freedom from craving and addiction—is easily within the reach of your new potential.

Like a child who first learns to ride a bike, a whole new world has opened up beyond your old limits. Explore. Enjoy.

And while you are out there, you can enhance the three essential virtues that make craving a thing of the past.

> **Toughness:** Radiating energy is particularly good for making you tougher, more resistant to the seductions of popular opinion and the cult of self-esteem. Remember that you are not only receptive to forces and ideas from outside yourself. You project power and can even affect the world around you. Your defenses are not easily breached.
>
> **Common Sense, Creativity, and Cleverness:** Exploring the sensations produced by life and movement can strengthen your command of the "three Cs" of intelligence. In so doing, you are dabbling with particularly animate energy fields. These should serve only to remind you that seemingly undetectable solutions are often waiting to be discovered. You didn't know what tremendous force resides within you and within all living things, and that should be a lesson to you. Many things become apparent, many problems yield up solutions when peered at by an active, intelligent mind.
>
> **Patience and Endurance:** The basic exercises for activating your Bio Energy are well suited to enhancing your patience and endurance. It will take both time and effort to master your Bio Energy. The daily practice will bring forth commitment and stick-to-

itiveness that you never suspected. The habit of dedicating yourself to these exercises will encourage more and more determination. Bio Energy is mastered slowly, with patience. You don't pop a pill to get it. It is the same with your cravings. The miracle cures always disappoint. Freedom is only achieved with patience and endurance.

There, you now have discovered a dramatic new tool. The potential of your Bio Energy is limitless. Believe me. I have spent the past three decades following this force, and I haven't stopped yet. I hope that you will spend many years more exploring your hidden sixth sense.

But, first we have today's work to do.

The next section of the book outlines the concrete tips and techniques that have helped tens of thousands of people kick their cravings.

The practical advice contained in the following chapters, if fully implemented with the Bio Energy you've just learned and the new attitude you're developing, can take you from a life of bondage to a life of freedom. Your prison will be no more.

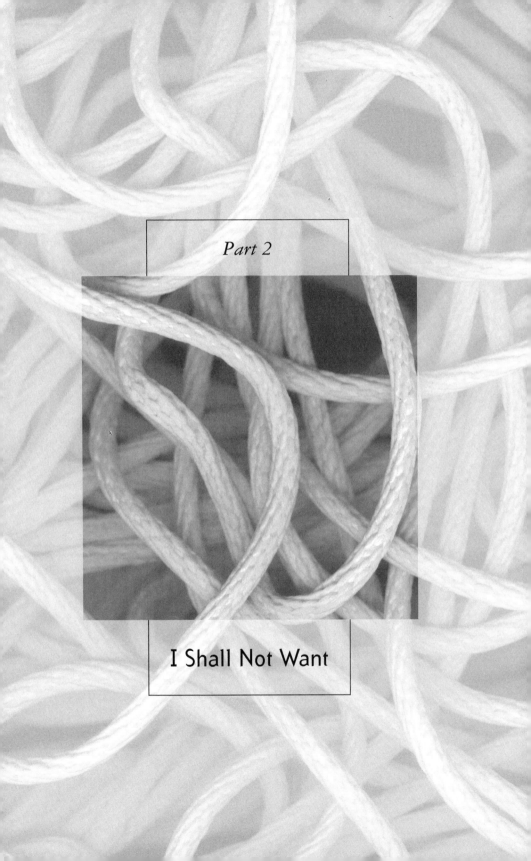

Part 2

I Shall Not Want

Chapter 8

Stopping Overeating:
The Tips and Techniques
Used in My Overeating Sessions

Who doesn't enjoy the taste of good food? Enjoy, yes. But *love?*

The first time I heard people blame love—either their love for food or the lack of love in their lives—rather than their own indugence or bad habits for being overweight was when I left the Soviet Union.

> **Y**ou have an innate desire to eat, but you don't have an innate desire for a particular food.

New theories about the causes for overeating appear in the media almost every day. One of the newest proclaims that the solution to overeating, or any addiction, for that matter, lies in bio-balancing the brain.

Overeating, according to this theory, is simply a sign that a certain neurotransmitter—serotonin—is missing in the brain. If a person has a constant craving for food (or alcohol or drugs), so this theory goes, even a mere deficiency of this neurotransmitter—serotonin—in that individual's brain is the source of the problem. I don't think so. I don't think it has anything to do with serotonin, not even a tiny little bit.

You want chocolate, for example, because you like chocolate, because you are used to liking chocolate, because you taught yourself to like chocolate. You crave potato chips, I assure you, not because there's something in your genetic code. There's no chemical missing in your brain that has destined you to a life devouring bag after bag of potato chips. It's not mysterious; what's not to like about chocolate or potato chips?

Here is an example drawn from my own life. When I lived in the Soviet Union, I never heard of anyone eating raw fish. Nobody did it, and I never thought of it, nor did I ever even dream I would ever do it. When I came to America, I discovered sushi. And to my surprise I thought it was marvelous, so marvelous, I could eat sushi all the time. It was so good that sometimes I even dreamed about it.

But I never even knew about it until I arrived in America. So is my taste for sushi, my craving for sushi genetic? Hardly. It's simply a matter of habit, of adaptation. And for me, it is totally within my control.

But I know there are many, many people who cannot control their particular cravings—be it for chocolate or potato chips or ice cream or cake, or sushi for that matter.

Men and women who have struggled all their lives with the problem of overeating have been helped by the techniques that follow. They can help you. I want you to have results forever. But you have to do what I say, 100%. If you do, you have to add these guidelines to the things you've already learned. You have to develop the three essential virtues and practice your Bio Energy.

If you do, you can lose. And you will do it:

Without diets.

Without restrictions.

Without counting calories.

Follow my guidelines and you can stop overeating—now and forever.

Shattering the Myths About Weight Loss

Several popular notions about weight loss are accepted as gospel, even by those who should know better. Many people who have unsuccessfully tried one diet after another still cling to some old standbys that seem to crop up on every diet. It's a wonder to me how these concepts reappear with each "revolutionary" diet and with every new "miracle" weight-loss program. Possibly, that's because no one has seriously questioned if they are truly effective methods of achieving weight loss.

These notions passing as truths are, in fact, only myths. I hope to dispel each one of them, so that they will not interfere with your goal of losing weight.

The Three Myths of Weight Loss

Myth #1: Drink ten glasses of water a day

Myth #2: Decide how much weight you want to lose and stick to it

Myth #3: Get on a diet and stick to it

Myth #1: The Water Myth

Contrary to almost every other diet that recommends drinking ten glasses of water a day, I want to show you why following this advice is crazy and self-defeating. If you accept this myth (remember, it's only posing as sound advice), you will be sorely disappointed. It will make you gain more weight.

I'm not against water, please understand. But it's important for you to recognize one critical fact. The stomach is very flexible, while water is not flexible at all. It's a scientific fact that water is physically incompressible. Therefore, if you drink a lot of water while you're trying to lose weight, what's the point? Your stomach will expand to make room for all this water. And the result? You'll end up with a much bigger stomach than you had before. And therefore, you'll wind up with a capacity for eating more food than you had, before you began your diet. So, once you get tired of drinking all that water—and you will—you'll end up being as fat as an elephant.

Here's my advice. Yes, you can drink water, but small amounts, sipped slowly. It's absolutely not necessary to force yourself to drink eight to ten glasses of water a day. Follow my advice, along with the other guidelines in this chapter, and after you've lost your desired weight *your stomach will be smaller, not larger, than it was before.*

Myth #2: Decide How Much Weight You Want to Lose and Stick to It

Don't get nervous, I'm not crazy, and I'm not against scales. It's important *not* to pick a specific number of pounds to lose. Your exact shape and exact weight have absolutely no connection. Muscle, after all, weighs more than fat.

Imagine if you were to take a piece of meat and a slab of saturated fat of the same size and place each of them on a scale. You'd discover that the meat, which is primarily muscle, will weigh more. So don't worry about your weight. If you are muscular, you may weigh more, but you'll have a better shape. Remember: *What you weigh or what you think you should weigh has nothing to do with how you look.*

Myth #3: Get on a Diet and Stick to It

To me this is utter nonsense. First of all, there is nothing magical or miraculous about losing weight. So no diet can promise you the miracle of losing weight and keeping it off forever. Why? The answer is simple:

The weight you lose with a diet will stay off *only* as long as you're on a diet, *only* as long as you live with a diet's restrictions. Therefore I *will not suggest a diet, because all diets work only as long as you're on them.*

Strategies, Tactics, and Weapons to Help You with the Battle

In an earlier chapter, I gave you the "rules of engagement" for the war you are waging against your cravings. Now we're into the specifics. So it's time for a briefing on strategies, tactics, and weapons.

Why It's Crucial Not to Eat Between Meals

I strongly recommend you eat nothing, absolutely *nothing,* in between meals. Not fruit, not vegetables, not soft drinks, not coffee, not diet soft drinks. You can only have water. But remember: sipped slowly and not in huge amounts.

For those of you used to snacking, it may feel natural to eat at numerous intervals throughout the day. It can seem as if "munching" is something you're born with—part of your genetic code, like the color of your eyes or hair. But I assure you, the desire to eat in between meals is no more inborn than a love of ice cream. Food cravings and the desire to eat in between meals are simply habits, adaptations, what you're used to doing.

Think of it this way. The brain is a computer, and you are the computer programmer. Only you have the power to change the patterns. You can reprogram the computer in your brain and teach it to ignore the instructions it sends to eat between meals, to munch and nibble whenever you think of it.

Apart from that, there are important health reasons why, unless you are a diabetic or suffering from some special health condition that requires frequent intake of food, you shouldn't eat in between meals.

Consider the most innocent snack.

The carrot.

An innocent vegetable. Of course, it looks innocent—this piece of carrot. It could even be celery. It's a snack without any junk, without any calories to speak of. So you may think it's a very innocent piece of vegetable.

I say, it's not so innocent. Why? You put it in your mouth, and the next second, the signal goes to your stomach: "Food coming!"

Why? Because the stomach is supposed to give you acid to help your body break down and digest the food. But if you have a bite of that innocent-looking carrot, the stomach makes acid, and that acid in your stomach is awaiting more food.

Think of that acid as looking around for a job. Its first job is to make you hungry for more food. But if you have a snack, a bite of that carrot, for example, and don't give your stomach any more food, the acid has nothing to do. It is left with only one job: to make trouble.

Besides, people who are accustomed to eating between meals are hungry all day long. If you are one of these people, think about it; you know I'm right.

The same is true of an animal. Anyone who's ever owned a dog or a cat knows that if you feed your pet twice a day, that is precisely what the animal will become accustomed to. He won't be running around, pawing you, barking or mewing, and whining for more food. But if you begin feeding him little snacks in between meals, the same cat or dog will begin pestering you all day long, expecting to get another treat.

Both the human body and the animal's body are very smart. And the human body doesn't ask for more calories than necessary. Even if you are used to snacking throughout the day, you can retrain yourself to change the pattern.

Try this: eat three meals a day for one week, with nothing in between, and you will see for yourself. You will lose the desire to eat in between meals for the rest of your life.

You don't think so?

Let me give you a perfect illustration. Again, I'll use the military as an example, but here I'm not speaking of battle plans, rather of the men and women who wage the battles.

For generations, the armies and navies of many countries call on the strongest, most active young men to serve their countries. In every case, in every country—be it Russia, Italy, or the United States—the military takes these young men (and increasingly women as well), takes even the most spoiled, most self-indulgent young men, men who are accustomed to eating whatever and whenever they want, and within a period of days retrains them to eat only three meals a day.

I repeat: I don't give a damn how spoiled the boy, after ten days in the service, he has adapted to three meals a day. And no problem. Moreover, these young men and women are far more active than most of us, burning up many more calories. This is a perfect illustration of the fact that eating habits are not genetic; they're only a matter of adaptation.

The human body seldom asks more than is necessary. But if you give it more, it'll accept. Why not? Let's say you already finished breakfast. Let's also say that I will give you a piece of cake, an unbelievably wonderful cake. You'll eat this cake. So would I. Why not? You physically can, of course, but it's not necessary. You're not hungry.

But, if you don't think about it, if you change the subject, think about the terrible weather, think about the work piled on your desk, if the cake isn't sitting there in front of you, it doesn't matter how good it is. If you throw the cake out, take the cake away, or don't have the cake in the house, it won't be there to tempt to you. That's it, once you change the subject and remove the trigger, it's gone from your life.

In the next chapter, read the section on changing the subject.

The point is very simple, don't dwell. Why create problems in an empty place?

How to Control Portions

Many people ask me, if you don't give me a diet—if you don't specify what to eat and how much to eat—how will I know what portions I can eat? And if I can't control the portions, how can I lose weight?

The answer is simple. Prepare whatever you're planning to have for your meal in advance. Before you eat one bite, set it all in front of you, from appetizer to coffee, and take a good hard look. Don't touch it—until you agree with yourself—not until you are 100% sure—that everything you see before you is not too much. Make damn certain that it won't make you feel guilty after you've eaten it.

At the same time, don't skimp. Eat a full meal. You are a machine, after all, and you need fuel to run. If you eat too small a meal, you'll be hungry all the time. You'll be snacking and all your attempts to lose weight will fail—and boom! This too will make you fat like an elephant.

After you decide what you will eat and remove everything that is too much or will make you feel guilty, what you see before you is what your meal will be. That's it. Nothing more. Nothing after. Nothing in between this meal and the next one.

In Praise of Vegetables

Whenever possible, at every meal, try to eat the vegetables first. The reason is quite simple. Vegetables fill up the stomach. If you begin your meal with them, the feeling of hunger quickly disappears. Your stomach is full, so the pangs of hunger are gone. If you begin your meal with vegetables or fruits, this means you're making your stomach full with almost no calories and still with plenty of nutrition.

Following my method, you're not supposed to count calories. It's very depressing and I don't like it. I don't think anybody likes it.

So try this: eat the vegetables first; after that, when you take a small piece of the fish or the meat, whatever, you'll feel completely comfortable. Full, even. Everything is OK and you won't be feeling guilty. Why? Because when you are ready to eat those other foods—fat and meat and bread, for example—you are less hungry and don't eat large amounts of these more fattening foods.

Using this technique, even the most indulgent people, those with the greatest craving for fats and sweets, will lose weight. In a sense, if you begin your meals by eating vegetables, they will function like the balloon that surgeons insert in the stomachs of very obese people to prevent them from overeating.

Another advantage to loading up on vegetables at the beginning of a meal is that they *are* compressible, unlike water. With vegetables, even if you eat a great deal of them, your stomach will not expand, it will remain normal.

Interestingly, many of you do this already quite naturally. Think how many times you begin your meal with a salad. You probably do this out of habit. Or remember the times you go to a party where a large buffet table is set out before you. Usually most of you begin with the vegetables before you select the meat or the fish. You now do this out of habit without thinking. In the future, I hope you will do it on purpose.

Eat Slowly—The Stomach Is Not a Computer

The brain, as we know, is a computer that both stores and transmits information about everything we think and feel. One piece of information it provides us is whether we're hungry or not. Whether we crave something or not.

Unlike the brain, the stomach is not a computer. It takes the stomach some time to get the idea that it's had enough food. It takes time to register the feeling that it's had enough.

The lesson for us is this: *Eat slowly.*

Give your stomach time to receive the food. Give it time to realize it's full. If you are patient, it will tell you.

March!

The weight you lose with exercise, with activity, is weight you lose forever. But the weight you lose with a diet will stay off *only* as long as you're on a diet, *only* as long as you live within a diet's restrictions.

Think of a soccer ball. This is the amount of food you eat in a single day. Now cut the soccer ball in half. That's how much you eat on a diet. As long as you're eating one half a soccer ball's worth of food, you're like a gazelle. Everybody's happy. But naturally, nobody wants to live on a diet forever. So you start eating the other half. Before long, the gazelle has become an elephant.

Therefore, don't diet. All diets work only as long as you're on them. Instead, exercise as much as possible.

I strongly recommend exercise for a very simple reason: There is only one way to lose weight fast—additional activity.

Even if you were to close your mouth completely and not touch any food for twenty-four hours, you wouldn't lose more than half a pound. Why? Because during the day we need 2,000 calories. And 2,000 calories is half a pound. That's it. It's not mystical. It's not a miracle.

And what about all those exotic diets that promise you'll lose fifty pounds in a week? It's my opinion that if you follow them, you can become an invalid for the rest of your life. You can destroy all your organs because it's very dangerous to lose that much weight in such a short time. There is only one safe way to increase weight loss: increase activity and exercise daily.

All exercise is good. However, I think swimming is the most beneficial form of exercise. Because of the resistance from the water, when you swim you use up more calories than running or bicycling. Without feeling you're pushing yourself, without exertion, you'll get more benefit in less time. An added bonus is that you won't beat up on your joints as you can in other forms of exercise.

Inevitably the question arises, "Is there a better time of day to exercise?"

I maintain that exercise is most beneficial in the morning. That is because morning exercise makes you feel better all day. Moreover, you won't have to fight the fatigue you might feel toward evening. Additionally, exercising early in the day will speed up your metabolism for the whole day. If you exercise early, you'll burn up more calories throughout the day.

You must exercise for more than twenty minutes. Science tells us that in the first twenty minutes, the human body destroys sugar, *not* fat. If you want to destroy fat, you must exercise longer than thirty minutes.

It doesn't matter how you do it, but move around for thirty minutes every morning. Isn't that better than spending a lifetime forever battling your weight, forever on a diet?

Of all the incentives to motivate you to exercise, not only while you are trying to lose weight but for the rest of your life, the following I think is the most powerful.

One million years ago if a man injured his leg, that meant he couldn't go out hunting or foraging for something to eat. His body stored fat until he was healthy. Because of this fact, he could survive. The body had nourishment to survive until he was healthy enough to be active again. Primitive man's body used this fat as emergency food. His fat cells were all that stood between him and death.

This information is in our genetic program. Fat cells survive with great persistence. They are more stubborn even than muscle. That's bad news.

This is the good news. When people are constantly active throughout their lives, their bodies know this as well. This information is recorded by their bodies, which now recognize that they don't have to collect all that extra fat. Their bodies have become educated. Their bodies know that because they are active, they'll always have adequate amounts of food.

But when you cut down activity, the body changes its metabolism. The body becomes careful with its calories, storing them for the future. It begins collecting fat, preparing for an emergency, the way it did for primitive man. So, what happens? A sedentary person's body is in a constant state of emergency.

If such a person, a person who has lived all along without activity, decides to begin exercising, he changes the pattern. The brain reprograms itself, and it tells the body to change its pattern. With this new program, it learns it doesn't need to store fat—the emergency is gone.

Look at this way. Let's imagine we're going on a trip to the Arizona desert. We'll bring along a bag of food and water. Once we arrive in Phoenix, there are restaurants, so we can drop our bags of food and water because we no longer need them. In the same way, when we no longer need stores of fat, our bodies adapt and shed it.

If your body is convinced that you're healthy and you don't need stores of fat for emergencies, it will begin shedding those reservoirs of fat. But you must do exercise *every* day for thirty minutes to convince the body *not* to store fat. You must tell your body that you are active and that food is always available. Otherwise, sirens go off, and the fat goes on.

This theory was developed by a doctor in Moscow who was a specialist at the most important institute for weight loss in Russia. After years of research, she concluded that *you must give your the body the message you're healthy and be active every day.*

Avoid Artificial Substitutes

For example, don't use artificial sweeteners instead of sugar. The human body has genetic information about everything around us, but it doesn't have it about substitutes. As life developed on this planet, and as we ourselves were growing up, sugar was everywhere. Many people who don't want to take sugar instead take this stuff in the pink-colored packages. Once in a while they should read what's written down in English on these packages. So ask yourself, if it's not sugar, what the hell is it?

You Don't Have to Give Up Anything, Any Category of Food

Since we're talking about sugar, this is a good time to tell you that it's unintelligent and unhealthy to remove any category of food. Don't give up *all* sugar or fat, *all* bread, or *all* fried foods.

Have a little bit; it's not a disaster. Life is supposed to be reasonable, after all.

This all-or-nothing attitude seems to me to be another peculiarly Western thing. Why? I think it has to do with TV. Many people in the West must watch TV the majority of their day. Whenever I call many of my patients, frequently the first thing they say is, "Can I turn down the TV?"

Midday, night, morning—it doesn't matter when I call, they're all watching TV. And what are they watching? They're watching TV commercials. And what do these commercials say? "I love cheese!" "I must give up sweets." "Cut out fats," etc.

This has come to become part of life, so when these people come to me they say, "I want to give up *all* fat, *all* fried food, *all* sugar."

It's quite ridiculous. To cut down is normal. To give up all sugar is ridiculous. Even diabetics cannot give up all sugar. To give up all bread means you give up fiber, essential B vitamins. To give up anything is ridiculous. Of course, it's possible and often preferable to give up a specific food like chocolate, for instance, if you have a deep craving for it. But to give up all sweets, all fats, I think is unhealthy and unwise. But, I know, the gods of public opinion disagree.

You've been briefed on the battle coming up. You're thinking like a soldier. You're familiar with your tactics and with your weapons. It's time to engage the enemy.

Orders of the Day

Here are your marching orders:
1. Eat a normal breakfast.
2. Eat your biggest meal in the middle of the day.

3. Eat the smallest meal of the day no less than four hours before going to sleep.
4. Exercise every day.

1. Eat a Normal Breakfast

Breakfast is the single most important meal of the day. Why? Because if you don't eat enough, you'll continue the pattern of eating in between meals. That, as I have demonstrated, is absolutely the worst thing you can do if you're trying to lose weight.

Eat a normal breakfast. Eat what is normal for *you,* not for somebody else. You will discover what is normal for you, your body, your activity. My definition of a normal breakfast is to eat enough. *Enough.* Not too much, but enough so that you will not be hungry, that you will not eat anything between breakfast and your midday meal.

The benefits of this method are critically important to anyone on a diet: no eating between meals means no stomach acid causing trouble and no thighs like a Russian weight lifter.

What I've just recommended, I know, is unlike any other diet in the world. But I mentioned in the beginning, I will give you no diet, no portions, and no calories to count. I'm sure you can remember, when you've been on a diet in the past, most diets give you the *exact* amount of *exactly* what you're supposed to have for breakfast. Six ounces of this, eight and a half ounces of that. Total calories consumed, etc. This is completely ridiculous, and I'll show you why.

Imagine a tall, youthful guy who's very active. He jogs before work, runs around an office all day long, dashes home, doing errands along the way, before going out for the evening. He probably doesn't get to sleep till midnight. And he's overweight.

Also imagine a short, sedentary, elderly lady who doesn't do anything but sit and watch TV all day. She goes to sleep before ten. She's also overweight.

Think about it. If they both ate the same size breakfast, in no time at all one would be terribly skinny the other terribly overweight. So you can see it's completely ridiculous to recommend the same diet for everybody.

I repeat because it's very important. *A normal breakfast is one that makes you feel satisfied without any desire to eat anything, until your next meal.*

But I know everybody wants to know *exactly* what to do. It's easier that way. So here is precisely what you should do each morning. Eat *enough* breakfast.

2. Eat Your Biggest Meal in the Middle of the Day

When I first came to the United States, I was surprised to discover that everyone ate their biggest meal at the end of the day. To me it seemed strange. In most countries in the world, the biggest meal is not eaten at night, but rather in the middle of the day. I'm not just talking about Russia, but many other countries, like Ireland, Italy, Austria, and Spain.

Let's imagine how people are used to eating in the United States. In America, your eating pattern looks something like this:

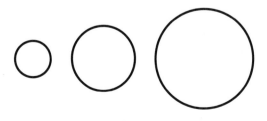

Notice, you go to bed on a full stomach. But instead follow the plan pictured here.

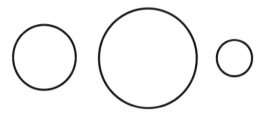

You'll go to bed on an empty stomach. While you're sleeping, your body will use up fat instead of calories, weight instead of food.

This is an old idea, and not mine personally. For example, the Italians, Spaniards, Germans, Irish, and Austrians eat their biggest meal in the middle of the day. The rest of the day is spent using up all this food for energy.

Why did the settlers who brought to the new land the habits and traditions of their native countries change this particular pattern? It seems to me that the answer to the question has nothing to do with the particular nutritional needs of Americans, but is rather historical.

America is a young country. More than two hundred years ago, when people came to America, it was a big empty place without villages or homes—without anything, really. Therefore, the people didn't have time to make the traditional big meals in the middle of the day. That was the time when they had to clear the land, hunt, and find animals to eat. So in the middle of the day, Americans had a small meal called lunch that they ate, instead of their traditional midday dinner.

It was only at nighttime, or sunset, that people got together for their big meal. At the end of the day when they returned from farming the land, clearing the brush, hunting the animals, they could take the time to prepare and enjoy their biggest meal of the day.

It evolved historically. A new tradition was created by the settlers. Having a big, heavy, family meal at the end of the day became the traditional way.

Traditional, for sure. American for sure. But today, it's no longer limited to Americans. Along with rock 'n' roll and blue jeans, people throughout Europe and other parts of the world are picking up this unfortunate habit of eating the American way. The industrialization of many countries, the demands of work, two-career families—social habits change. Today, the American habit of having the biggest meal at the end of the day is one of its most successful exports. But I maintain, *it's not healthy!*

An important reminder: whatever meal you're having, remember one of the first and most important ideas I gave you earlier. Before you sit down to eat, take everything you're going to have in a meal and place it before you. Look at it carefully and make sure it's enough. Enough, but not too much. Be absolutely certain that it's enough, that it's all you're going to eat, and you won't feel guilty after you've eaten it.

What about when you're dining out? How can you follow this plan in a restaurant? The answer is simple. When the waiter brings you your food, look at it carefully. If you think it's too much, ask the waiter to take away whatever you don't want or whatever you think will be too much, *immediately.* Don't leave it on your plate.

If it's not there, you won't eat it.

Because I don't recommend a specific diet, I'm always asked, "What can I eat at my biggest meal of the day? If you just say *anything,* I know I'll eat anything and *everything,* and I'll never lose weight."

Just because I don't give you a diet, I'm not saying you can eat *anything* or *everything.* The word I always use is *reasonable.* When you sit down for your largest meal of the day, eat reasonably.

What is reasonable for one person may not be reasonable for everyone. But, generally, this means you can have a salad, but not necessarily one filled with croutons or topped with mounds of a rich cheese dressing. You can have some vegetables, for sure. Potatoes, or some other starch of some kind, and perhaps a piece of meat or chicken or fish. You can even order dessert. The point is, if you've started with some vegetables, eaten your meal slowly, and given your stomach the time it needs so that you feel you've had enough, you won't even be able to eat much of the dessert anyway.

Take your time when you eat. We're not out hunting and fishing and clearing the brush anymore. So whatever meal you're having, remember to take the time to eat slowly.

> **Y**ou can eat reasonably and not gain weight.

3. Eat the Smallest Meal of the Day No Less Than Four Hours Before You Go to Sleep

The last meal of the day should be the smallest. The smaller, the better, and the more dramatic your weight loss will be. Have nothing, *zero,* after that final meal of the day. Be sure to have it no less than four hours before going to sleep.

If you follow my plan, at the end of the day you will have spent all the calories you've consumed. You will go to sleep with a practically empty stomach. If your body needs any calories, it will take them from your body. In that case, you'll be using up stored fat, rather than food, losing weight rather than calories from your stomach.

When you're sleeping you don't feel hungry just like you don't feel pain during surgery.

4. Exercise Every Day

Remember, you have to send your body an important message every day. You have to tell your body you are an active person and there's no reason to save reservoirs of fat for an emergency. There is no emergency. Teach your body to burn up fat on a regular basis, and the only way to do it is by daily exercise.

Also remember, if it's necessary to get up a half hour earlier to do your exercises, so be it. Wouldn't you prefer to lose a half hour of sleep each night? Or would you rather spend years on diets?

Do you want to be fat and sleeping rather than awake and gorgeous?

Your Battle Cries

No soldier can go into the heat of battle without a primal yell to keep the spirits up. Here are yours:

Remind yourself, being skinny doesn't mean you're beautiful.

A skinny cow is not a gazelle.
Food is not love.
Losing weight is a matter of willpower and discipline.
There is no magic potion, diet, or medication.
Diets work only when you live with their restrictions.
Exercise every day for at least thirty minutes.

Most people who come to my office to stop overeating want to leave with a diet—a piece of paper that tells them what they can and cannot eat. Instead of a diet, I give them a poem. This poem will help them more than any diet on the market. The poem is called "If" and it's by Rudyard Kipling. Here are a few lines from it.

> If you can keep your head when all about you
>   are losing theirs and blaming it on you.
> If you can trust yourself when all men doubt you
>   and make allowance for their doubting, too. . . .
>   If you can meet with Triumph and Disaster
>   And treat those two imposters all the same. . . .
>   If you can fill the unforgiving minute
>   With sixty seconds worth of distance run,
>   Yours is the Earth and everything in it.

Chapter 9

Stopping Smoking:
The Tips and Techniques
Used in My Smoking Sessions

In the last chapter, I told you that losing weight is like a war. It is. Learning the attitudes and attributes of a good soldier is only the beginning. You must learn tactics, the intricacies of your weapons, and courage. Then you must march into battle and stick with the fight until the war is won.

Stopping smoking is different. It's not a war. It's more like hand-to-hand combat. It's something you train for, for sure. You learn and practice. You become a warrior in thought and deed.

You must put all that you've learned into a quick burst of power. In a matter of moments, the struggle is over. You've vanquished your opponent.

In this chapter, I will give you your final pep talk before the battle.

You are already a warrior with the three virtues and your Bio Energy. Now, it is time to learn a few basic techniques. Use them all, use them fast, and remember that you have no time for mistakes.

It's time to defeat smoking. In *this* battle, it's kill or be killed.

Robert Rienzi is a highly successful executive in Boston—successful in almost everything he touched. But he had one problem. His addiction to smoking had defeated him time and again. In his work he made countless business deals that involved millions of dollars—mergers, acquisitions, corporate buyouts. But he had been unable to close the one deal he most eagerly wanted. He could not stop smoking.

He had stopped and started again at least twenty times. He was sharing his predicament with others seated in the large semicircle in my office, and I noticed how they nodded their understanding. Like Robert, it seemed that they, too, despite the other achievements they had been able to attain in their lives, had been unable to break their craving for cigarettes.

I remembered an ancient fable that seemed perfect for the occasion and began the session with that story. As Robert would tell me months later, when the victory over his addiction to cigarettes was finally won, and this ancient story had great meaning for him. I think it will work for you as well.

Hundreds and hundreds of years ago, in a small Middle Eastern country there was a hero who I will call Ali. Like Robin Hood, he used to take from the rich and tried to help the poor.

One day he came before the Sultan and said, "Look, in your jails you have locked up many people who didn't pay taxes. But don't you see, as long as they're in jail they cannot pay taxes anyway, because they cannot work in jail. So what is the reason to keep them there?"

The Sultan said, "It may be a good idea to give them freedom, but if I do, afterward nobody will pay their taxes because nobody will be afraid *not* to pay taxes."

Ali replied, "Of course, you're right, but I want to make a deal with you."

"What kind of deal?" the Sultan asked suspiciously.

"I will make you the richest person in the world, if you'll give freedom to those people," Ali told the Sultan.

The Sultan thought for a moment and asked, "How will you make me so rich?"

"Simple," Ali replied confidently. "Everything you touch will turn to pure gold, absolutely pure gold. You'll have anything, everything you want. There is one small condition, but it's no big deal."

The Sultan asked, "What's the condition?"

"In the moment when you touch something, anything, don't think about a white monkey."

"What the hell are you talking about?" the Sultan replied. "I never thought about a white monkey in my entire life!"

So they made the deal. The Sultan gave the order, and the jails were opened. Once all the people were freed, he told Ali, "OK, do it."

And Ali replied, "I already did it, just follow my instructions and you will now be the richest man in the world."

Of course, the Sultan began thinking only about the white monkey and nothing else and, as a result, nothing turned to gold. Why? Because he was told *not* to think about it. That's human mentality.

The same thing happens when a person quits smoking. He immediately starts thinking about the damn smoking. Why? Because smoking is much more than a process where you take a cigarette and inhale and exhale and inhale again. It's connected unconsciously to countless activities and emotions.

In my smoking sessions, I never talk about the dangers of smoking. Why? Because if the people are attending my lectures, they are *already aware* of the dangers. Just as you, reading my book, already know the dangers of smoking, or else you wouldn't be reading this chapter in the first place.

Once you've made the decision to stop, in order to really break free of your addiction to nicotine you will need to call on the same vital weapons I've mentioned earlier—inner toughness; common sense, creativity, and cleverness; and patience and endurance. In this chapter, you'll find the same guidelines I give people in my office. These can help you and give you the support you need to keep you away from smoking.

Without Pills
Without Patches
Without Gum
Without Substitutions
Without Weight Gain

I want to show you how to get great results without negative side effects. For the vast majority of people, the worst side effect of giving up smoking is weight gain. So I will show you how you can stop smoking without adding pounds and inches. It's those pounds and inches that inevitably drive newly reformed smokers right back into the habit they are trying so desperately to conquer.

I've met thousands of people who have tried to stop smoking and gained huge amounts of weight in the process, so I know all too well how terribly they feel. They come away from the experience not only with a sense of failure, but overweight. Disheartened, they are also under the delusion that among nicotine's wondrous powers is the ability to burn away fat. So what do they do? Naturally, they go back to smoking. It's a cycle that happens again and again, and it is ultimately what drives many of them to my office.

Despite all the myths, it is physically impossible for nicotine to kill fat—if it were true, all smokers would be emaciated or dead. All smokers would be melted down to nothing.

There are three principal reasons why people gain weight when they stop smoking. Once these are understood, I'll show you how to deal with all of them.

Food Tastes Better

After you stop smoking, food tastes better. Why? Physically, nicotine represses taste. So when you stop smoking, your tongue is more sensitive; suddenly food tastes marvelous! If food tastes better, it's natural for you to want a second piece of cake or another piece of cheese. And it's also natural that, like most people, you don't want a second piece of broccoli.

Instead of even thinking about a second portion of food, try to eat one tablespoon less at each meal. Do it every day; soon it will become a habit.

Don't Replace the Cigarette

The second reason for weight gain when you stop smoking is that it's natural to replace the cigarette with a substitute. In fact, many systems designed to help people stop smoking emphatically recommend that you have something *instead* of the cigarette.

Give up the notion of having something, anything, instead of the cigarette. By that, I mean zero substitutes: no candy, gum, fingers, pencils, or soft drinks. Water is acceptable, and you may drink small amounts of water when you wish. But not *instead* of a cigarette. Ignore the popular and widely held belief that having a glass of water every time you want a cigarette will help you through the pangs of withdrawal.

Eliminate the Notion of "Instead"

There is a powerful reason for my admonition not to do anything *instead* of smoking. Even an "innocent" glass of water, when taken instead of a cigarette, can interfere with your successfully giving up smoking.

Since this advice doubtlessly flies in the face of everything you've ever heard about stopping smoking, let me explain. Whenever you do something—anything—instead, even taking a glass of juice or diet soda or that apparently innocent glass of water, it only becomes a reminder of what you're trying to give up.

Recommending zero substitutions is at the heart of my stop-smoking program. If you follow this advice scrupulously, it will make it easy for you to give up smoking successfully without gaining weight.

Remember, your brain is a computer. You are the computer programmer. If you don't put anything in your mouth *instead* of a cigarette for ten days, you will reprogram your brain. But if you suck on a hard candy, munch a few pretzels, or chew on a pencil, the old program is still alive and well. Pretty soon you'll either gain enormous amounts of weight from all that snacking and munching, or you'll be smoking again. Why? Because if you constantly send, "Food coming!" messages to your body, the acid begins to churn as the stomach prepares to receive more food. This will only succeed in making you even hungrier than if you had eaten nothing at all. Besides, all this acid floating around your stomach can be a real troublemaker and cause real problems for your health. So, no snacks!

As for water? I repeat. I am not the Mad Russian. I have nothing against water. But don't drink large amounts of it *instead* of smoking. Remember water is incompressible. So, downing large amounts of it will make your stomach expand. You'll end up with a capacity for greater amounts of food than you had before you stopped smoking. A good way to gain weight, for sure.

You can learn this new program of not substituting for smoking. It's simply adaptation and not unlike learning to drive. Remember when you first learned to drive. You had to think about shifting gears. At first, you couldn't drive and talk at the same time. You had to concentrate, think only about shifting gears. So it is with smoking. If you have absolutely nothing—no snacks, no soda, no gum, no candy—instead of the cigarette, in a short time it will become automatic, and in time, you won't even have to think about it.

When I say zero, I'm including nicotine in any form—gum, patches, or drops. So, I repeat, I recommend no substitutions when you stop smoking.

Dwelling

Smoking has been a large part of your life; don't be scared if it comes to your mind.

Smoking is associated with so many parts of your life, with almost every aspect of your life: after eating, when you're depressed, when you're upset, when you want to relax, when you want to think about something, when you want to interrupt a conversation with someone else, when you need to give yourself a boost, and when you're talking to somebody who asks you a crazy question, you inhale, you give yourself a few more seconds.

Admit to yourself, if you haven't already, that smoking has clearly been a huge part of your life. It's associated unconsciously with things you do every day. When you quit, you change your life dramatically. If you don't think about it, it won't be difficult, but if you start to dwell on it, soon it will drive you crazy. Why? Because for years you have adapted to the cigarette. Of course, you'll think about it. It will enter your mind. How could it not?

Anyone who's trying to quit talks about nothing but smoking. But promise yourself you won't discuss it. Not discussing it means not complaining, not seeking out either commiseration or compliments. If you keep talking about it, it will never leave your mind. Not thinking about it will help you adapt to being a nonsmoker. Adaptation is the key; it's a true human trait. No adaptation, no advance. Humans are very gifted. With adaptation, you can make the impossible possible.

When you give up smoking, if you replace it with something else, as I've suggested, it's a form of self-sabotage. Every time you do "something else," it will only remind you of smoking. It's pointless to have a piece of gum whenever you want to smoke.

Soon, every time you see gum, your brain will go to smoking. The computer program is still intact, and just as you did all the years you smoked, you'll begin to feel that old hunger for a cigarette. The feeling will intensify and in no time you'll be puffing away. It's the same with the patch. These "aids" do a great job of keeping the addiction alive. *Unless you make the adaptation, the old addiction will return.*

Imagine a situation that seems to have nothing to do with smoking. It's like being in a second marriage and having a picture of your former spouse in every room—in the kitchen, in the dining room, in the bedroom. So, every time you walk in that room, it's impossible *not* to think of that person. It's natural.

Or imagine, your lover leaves you, and you're devastated. If you leave pictures all around the house, or if you walk in the neighborhood where she lives, or if you go to her favorite restaurant— how will you ever forget that person? That's what the gum does. That's what the patch does. That's what a snack does. That's what water does. That's even what a pencil does!

> # No reminders, no obsessions.

So when you stop smoking, my advice:

Don't substitute.
Don't dwell.
Change the subject.

A Reminder About Weight Gain

Nothing causes former smokers to return to their addiction faster than gaining weight. So when you stop smoking, it's essential to follow the guidelines for weight loss scrupulously: review the material in Chapter 8.

How to Combat the Common Withdrawal Symptoms of Dizziness or Insomnia

Fifteen minutes of exercise before breakfast will help you break the sometimes troubling symptoms associated with withdrawal from nicotine.

Exercise improves your blood circulation. This is of utmost importance. When you smoked, you reduced that circulation and reduced the amount of oxygen going through your blood vessels. Now that you've stopped, there's no nicotine racing around your system closing up your arteries, but your heart is still pumping away, just as it always did. Is it any wonder you get headaches and dizziness?

But exercise is the best answer to that problem, especially in the morning. It opens up your blood vessels to their full extent. When you exercise, you're preparing your body for this increased circulation that it will experience all day long after you stop smoking.

Exercising in the morning has another benefit as well—it raises your energy level and enhances your peace of mind for the whole day. If you're more active, more focused, and more at peace, it's going to be even easier for you to put smoking out of your mind.

When you are living, as you will be, in the moment, your mind won't be cycling about idly, just waiting for that old cigarette urge to creep back in. Also, the physical well-being you feel will help counter the effects of dizziness and insomnia.

I recommend doing exercise and increasing your physical activity as a means of controlling your weight when you give up smoking. But I must offer one caveat. If you are doing the exercise with the grim determination that you're doing it instead of smoking, it won't work. It will not be successful. That's simply because you will still be thinking of smoking. And before long, more than just thinking.

So my advice: exercise to feel better; exercise for your health; exercise because it speeds up your metabolism. Don't exercise *instead* of smoking.

Now I want to ask you, for a moment, to address another problem. It is an exercise, and it will take some concentration. It is an exercise I do in my sessions with patients and I'd like to share it with you.

Please look at the following painting.

Does it seem familiar?

Have you seen it before?

I'll give you a clue, it is a portrait of a famous European.

Still, don't recognize her?

She was one of the great monarchs of all time.

Not French. No, not Italian.

And not Spanish.

No idea? Look at it again.

Sorry, time's up. That's it!

Actually, it doesn't matter if you thought it was Queen Victoria or Cleopatra or Queen Isabella. The point is that in the middle of reading about how to stop smoking, you actually stopped thinking about smoking for a few minutes.

For the record, it's a picture of Catherine the Great.

Changing the Subject

When you stop smoking, it is essential to change the subject. For a smoker, this often seems impossible. But in our lives each of us is able to change the subject when we have to. I just proved it. But how about something not so dramatic, something ordinary?

Each of us knows that someday we will be dead. Yet we continue going to work, pursuing our goals, loving each other, raising our children—that is to say, we go on with our lives. Because who the hell could stand constantly thinking about death, knowing it could come tomorrow, next week, or many years in the future? You'd go crazy!

If you can go on with your life with the knowledge, the certainty, that someday, like everyone else's, your life will end, if you can change the subject about your own death, you can also change the subject about smoking. Compared to death, smoking seems pretty easy.

Remember Lisa who's job was so stressful she felt she would never be able to control her addiction to cigarettes, never be able to stop smoking without gaining weight? I received a letter from her recently in which she told me that my system had worked.

There was one phrase that had helped her the most. She said she repeated it to herself every day. It worked for Lisa as it has for thousands of others who have come to me for help in their battle against cigarettes. In this book, I've written this phrase time and time again. I repeat it for you now, and as you wage your own battle against smoking, I ask that you repeat it every day. It is the basis of the no-substitutions argument.

> # What you're thinking, this is what your life will be.

In the following chapter, I'll show you how all the weapons in my arsenal are required to free yourself from a group of problems that are, in some ways, uniquely problems in the West, particularly problems in highly developed nations.

Arising out of the riches and abundance of the Western industrialized world, there is a complex of problems, many of which are unknown in other, less developed parts of the world. But troublesome they are, and, like the more familiar addictions, they can be a painful, sometimes heartbreaking affliction for everyone.

These thoughts can be so stubbornly entrenched that they seem to be inherited. Although my thinking is often viewed as unconventional, I think these problems are really indulgences, behavior that is self-inflicted and self-defeating.

But if any of these problems are restricting *your* freedom, or if they afflict anyone close to you, you'll need all your powers to defeat them.

Chapter 10

Diseases of Affluence: Cravings and Addictions in a Land of Plenty

Like millions of people, you may derive great inspiration and energy from being part of a society with a sense of boundless opportunity, where life is seen as a fountain of riches. But each of us knows that the same prospect—living in a land of perpetual plenty—has for some individuals a less benign, sometimes unfortunate, and even tragic dimension.

The results? I see them every day in my office—casualties of the dream machine of success. In the Soviet Union, I lived in a land where nothing made sense. So in the West, I also see things that make no sense. When I first left Moscow, it was my impression that the richness of opportunity and unrivaled standard of living in the West—while wonderful and admirable—had an unexpected side effect. They made citizens a bit more vulnerable to the shifting winds of public opinion, and a little bit spoiled. They have had another effect that falls into the category of what some people call the "Law of Unintended Consequences"—diseases of affluence.

It's important to acknowledge them for what they are: self-destructive forms of behavior. And the source? Unrealistic expectations. Within this broad category, there are countless variations. I've seen for myself the different manifestations these diseases of affluence can take. You may see yourself or recognize someone you care about as I outline this set of problems. If you do, rest assured, these can be solved using all the powers you have developed. What are diseases of affluence? They are the complaints you hear every day in our thriving society. Compulsive shopping, for example. Workaholism and sex addiction; the medicalizing of undesirable behavior.

All of the men and women that I see are seeking relief. For some, it's the vague, gnawing pain of feeling powerless, unable to change their own lives. Others, are stuck, caught in a web of chronic and self-defeating behavior. Too many are driven by the tyranny of knowing something is robbing them of their autonomy. Some are consumed by cravings for food or smoking; others are driven by different kinds of cravings and feel hopelessly locked at an impasse in their lives.

You may wonder what *they* are seeking from me. I'll tell you what they answer when I ask them. Looking ahead, they see a future that looms as impossible; looking back, all they can see is the litter of broken promises they have made to themselves and to their family and friends.

They see all their failed attempts at breaking patterns of behavior that, while not obviously self-destructive, stifle their capacity for finding joy, either in their work or in their personal lives. I know that feeling impotent to make changes in your own life doesn't mean you're self-destructive. But because this feeling often leads to self-defeating behavior, to me, it's a close call. I call it the path to self-destruction.

With the future terrifying and the past a wreck of failed intentions, what remains for many of the people I see is the present. But the present exists, not in a joy-of-seizing-the-moment sense. Instead, they experience a panicky, urgent insistense of the here and now—the gnawing desire to break out of the patterns of their lives. The present is about being trapped. Imprisoned.

I've developed another tool that has been highly effective with many men and women I have treated. It's involves a most unusual way of dealing with some of life's thornier problems. Unusual, yes, but as many former patients will attest, this approach requires neither thousands of dollars nor countless hours spent in a psychiatrist's office, sifting through the pains of childhood.

I've seen people manage to get their lives back on track. Perhaps for the first time in their lives, armed with new powers of control within themselves, they no longer are slaves to their addictions.

Some former patients have told me that this form of healing wasn't exactly what they expected when they made that first phone call to the Russian healer of Brookline. I can say equally for me as well, it wasn't the kind of healing I expected to become engaged in, nor is it something I studied at Popov's Laboratory in Moscow. It's a technique I learned later, creating it out of necessity, after I left the Soviet Union.

Broadening the Scope of Treatment

Over the years, I have encountered growing numbers of people who presented me with a new set of problems. People began seeking my advice on matters outside of the realm of physical pain. Every day, I seemed to be hearing stories of lives at an impasse, of families fracturing, of dreams deferred or ultimately denied. I heard for myself the stories of men and women feeling imprisoned even as they lived in the heart of the free world.

Each day I listened to people voicing similar anxieties. I could see how these anxieties were reflected in unhealthy cravings and fueling even more serious addictions, so I began to focus on new ways of helping them.

From a Land of Scarcity to a Land of Plenty

I am, I concede, someone who spent forty years in a world where paucity and scarcity were the norm, where the grayness and predictability of limited horizons were the stuff of everyday life. After forty years of life under Soviet Communism, I'm still dazzled by how much the images of affluence and abundance are essential parts of the emotional landscape of the free world.

Possibly *your* own emotional landscape is filled with these images without your even knowing it. Westerners seem to have absorbed them, as if they had become essential elements in the atmosphere, inhaling them with each breath they take. It is, of course, that very picture of abundance and freedom, the prospect of a life lived with a richness of opportunity, that drew me and my family to begin life anew in the West. Perhaps it is the fact that I came from a country where abundance was unknown, and a lack of choices was the norm, that makes me so sensitive to the dizzying abundance I discovered outside the Soviet Union.

I cannot tell you how many people come to me as self-described workaholics. To me this is totally a problem for people in industrialized nations. Only in the West is the desire to work hard seen as an addiction.

When I think of life in the Soviet Union, I can't conceive of a single person visiting a doctor because they thought they were addicted to their work. As a rule, people hated their work, and if they worked hard, it was because they had to.

The notion that opportunities for advancement are all around us can have the perverse effect of fueling anxieties in many of the people I see.

Similar to millions of people, you may be spurred on by this picture of boundless opportunity and find the inspiration you need for achievement and the fulfillment of your dreams.

The picture of a life of affluence as being perpetually available, in easy reach, often turns out to be less of an inspiration than an illusion. In the same way the Soviet propaganda machine fed us a steady diet of what were essentially "Wonders of Communism infomercials," in the free world of the West, quick-fix infomercials and get-rich schemes are pitched to the public twenty-four hours a day.

And the message? It's simple. Four easy payments of eighty-nine dollars and fifty cents, and they'll send you the recipe. A bit of effort and a dash of pluck, and a few spoonfuls of risk. But, of course, the truth is that many people, even if they *have* the recipe, are unable to fill in all the ingredients of this glowing picture for themselves. Not only do they feel disillusioned, but flawed and filled with pain—the pain of failure.

I've seen countless cases where this pain is then transformed into endless cravings that become life-consuming addictions, as well as depressive behavior. Oscar Levant, the brilliant but tortured American pianist and writer, who knew both addiction and depression all too well, and whose life was cut short by a combination of both, put it best when he observed, "It's not what we are, it's what we didn't *become* that hurts."

The seeds of diseases of affluence can be found everywhere in a thriving society. But the fact is that these disorders are very costly to bear—costly to the person who's afflicted, costly to loved ones, and costly to the society itself.

However you measure it—whether in the millions of dollars seeking treatment, or the hours of pain, the lost hours at work, or the years wasted in the pursuit of empty dreams—the cost can be so great, it's a wonder to me that these problems aren't seen for what they are. Illnesses we cannot afford to indulge, illnesses too expensive to endure, especially when they're not illnesses at all.

Instead of considering this neutral, sober view of such afflictions, today the pervasive attitude is to nourish the belief that these are truly medical problems, maladies afflicting millions of people.

I've watched as an expanding universe of experts has been created to help the newly afflicted. Spinning out of this world is an industry generating millions of dollars each year. However flimsy the proof, the case made by its proponents is that these "diseases" are biological in nature. In fact, armies of people appear to be convinced that they're suffering from a biological malady, when the evidence seems clear that in many cases they're not biological.

Why are these "victims" and their "defenders" so eager to convince us that diseases of affluence are medical, as they stake their claims to new territories of illnesses?

The answer is simple once you consider some of the "benefits" of believing you're suffering from a biological malady. First, the biological diagnosis strips you of any responsibility or control over your behavior. However self-indulgent you may be, or selfish, or hurtful to others—*it's not your fault.* A genetic excuse is always easier to accept than taking responsibility for your own behavior.

Unhappy Kings and Happy Shoemakers

The media's infernal images perpetuate the notion that for a man to be considered really a man, he must be a success and, therefore, highly ambitious. Women must be successful on an increasing number of fronts, requiring that they, too, must be highly ambitious. To prove he's a man, he must succeed. She must prove she's a superwoman. What does this mean? This means each of them works eighty hours a week.

I see this every day. People come to my office, asking me questions about work all the time. "Can you give me the energy to work more?" "Can you take away the guilt I feel when I want to work less?" "What can I do? I have to smoke because my work makes me tense. And if I'm tense, I won't succeed." Or "I guess I overeat because I'm not the success I dreamed I'd be. So how can I ever stop eating?" "Why have I failed my own expectations?"

In the pages that follow, drawing from the experiences of people I've treated, I'll include several examples that reveal how this set of problems was resolved when these dark areas became flooded with light.

Even if the situations don't exactly mirror issues that concern you, take the time to read them. Think of them as mental exercises, another form of mental karate. You can refashion them to fit your own particular needs.

The anecdotes I mention throughout this book can be used as wake-up calls for troubled psyches.

One former patient wrote to tell me of the power these anecdotes held for her, comparing them to capsules that are swallowed but work on a delayed, sustained-release basis. For her and others, my stories have had an enduring value. Like time-release pills, the bits of philosophy and logic they contain can remain effective hours after ingestion. They possess a staying power strong enough to work their way through your mind, months after you've read them, strong enough to make your sense of freedom permanent and secure.

There's a thread running through these examples, which you can apply to the tapestry that is your life. It may involve a brand-new way of treating lifelong problems, but I promise, it's worth a try.

A man I'll call Ben Winters arrived at my office about a year ago. It was an icy March evening, and I recall that for some time he sat in my office, saying nothing for quite a while. After I inquired about why he continued to smoke, he pronounced, gloomily, "I'm not happy."

Looking at him, except for his sad eyes and down-turned mouth, I could tell he was OK. Well dressed, with a shine on his shoes, he didn't seem as if he'd given up caring for himself, as some people do when their spirits are low.

"What's the matter?" I asked.

"Smoking," he said as he finally slipped out of his coat and tossed it on the empty chair beside him. "Smoking, that's why I'm here."

"No, I mean, what's making you so unhappy?" I asked, studying his expression, looking for a sign that he could be sufficiently engaged to really open up to me.

He replied with an edge to his voice, "I'm not a very prestigious person, and I want to be more active, more aggressive. I want to be a financial success. Can you do this?"

"Absolutely not. First of all, if you wanted to be a financial success, you wouldn't need me to do it. You'd already be active and aggressive," I said.

"Second, even if I pulled off this miracle and made you a big success, you still might not be so happy. Public opinion tells you that you want position and prestige. But you have to decide if that's what public opinion wants, or what you want. Because, if you get it, it doesn't guarantee anything—including happiness."

Ben shook his head in disbelief. "Mr. Shubentsov, there I have to disagree. If I could have one thing that would make me happy, I know it would be a prestigious position."

Remembering the anecdote I mentioned earlier in this book, I told Ben the story about Napoléon Bonaparte, concluding with the line that would happily haunt Ben's thoughts for months. "If one of the most famous and powerful leaders in the history of the world could write at the end of his life that he enjoyed only six happy days, there is the best proof."

"Maybe you're right about Napoléon," Ben observed through a thin smile, "but that's not me. Napoléon must have been nuts."

"Nuts, maybe. But he wasn't alone," I told him. "No one ever got happiness from medals or decorations, position or prestige. It's ridiculous. This isn't my idea. A very smart guy named William Shakespeare said it best when he wrote, 'I used to see many unhappy kings and many happy shoemakers.' "

Ben grinned in spite of himself. After our session ended, Ben muttered, as he headed for the door, "Unhappy kings, Shakespeare said that? Not bad, I like it."

As we shook hands at the top of the staircase, I added, "Ben, you'll forgive me if I say, this is all American bullshit. I'm terribly sorry. Because to be prestigious is up to you. Do you want? Go ahead. You don't? Don't! You will be happy anyway. Prestige has nothing to do with happiness, not even a tiny little bit."

"Happiness," I added, "is when a person can wake up in the morning and enjoy going to work, and at the end of the day, be content with the notion that he's going home. That's it, simple. No miracles. Freud said it very simply, 'love and work.' "

Several months later, Ben phoned to tell me he had finally beaten his addiction to nicotine. He didn't know if it was my Bio Energy treatment or what he laughingly called my "Shakespeare Bonaparte Cure" that did it. I told him I thought it was probably a combination of the two.

Ben hadn't been promoted in his current job, he explained, but that hadn't thrown him. He thought our talk had prepared him for that possibility. But after receiving word about another position in a different company, he had just completed what he thought was a positive interview with a headhunter.

And his attitude about his prospects for the new job? He admitted the change in his mood was strange but wonderful to him. If he got it, fine. If not, not.

We chatted about how he had been caught up in what he called the "success trap," how easy it is in a society of such affluence to internalize aspirations and values that are almost impossible to achieve. It was the tension between the two—Ben's *own* values and the voice of public opinion, the values depicted in the infernal dream machine—that provided fertile territory for his unhappiness, as well as his smoking habit. Like millions of people, his smoking was a way of self-medication, treating that unhappiness with a drug. In his case, nicotine.

Other Diseases of Affluence

Chronic Shopping

Turn on the television, almost any time of the day or night. Open a magazine or a newspaper, any day of the week. It's inescapable. Hour after hour, and page after page are devoted to demonstrating to a hungry and vulnerable audience that thousands of people have found their way to the road to recovery. Recovery from what? From an ever-expanding number of addictions. To my way of thinking, some of these are not really addictions at all. But many people view these afflictions as diseases requiring medical or psychological intervention.

Consider the case of the chronic shopper, for example, whose credit card bills have escalated to such a degree that she can no longer pay the rent. I met one woman in my office who fell into this category; I'll call her Sally Bryant.

At fifty-two, Sally was divorced, and her job as a paralegal in a Boston law office didn't pay enough to support her particular craving—an insatiable desire to shop. When I first met her—a friend brought her to my office—she was facing a desperate situation. Her life of chronic spending had caught up with her.

Through bursts of tears, she told me that despite her compulsion to spend, she had managed to evade serious repercussions in the past. This time, however, she knew she was in deep trouble. She had failed to make the last six mortgage payments to the bank on the small house she lived in with her daughter, Sharon. She had no doubt that the bank would act on the threat she had received from them in the mail the week before: either come up with the money or be prepared to lose the house.

To top it all, she said, she was only sixteen months away from paying off the mortgage. Then she would own the house free and clear. Now she was facing the humiliating prospect of forfeiting the money she had carefully put aside for her daughter's education. Or else she would lose the house; that was the only option available to her.

Objectively, Sally's license to give in to her cravings, her inability to tame her chronic impulse to spend, had been a soul-crushing act of self-indulgence. In the past, Sally might have been seen as self-indulgent and irresponsible. But no longer. Today, she and millions of women and men like her are perceived as victims. Victims of what, you might ask. The answer is simple: victims of our old friends, "lack of self-esteem" or a "lack of love in early childhood"—the litany goes on and on.

No longer seen as self-indulgent, the shopaholic is said to be suffering from a disorder. Perhaps it's the Mad Russian in me or the sober view that an outsider brings to the table of diseases of affluence, but I have an entirely different take on those people who cannot stop spending or shopping.

I don't search for the seeds of such behavior in the ancient history of Sally's childhood. I don't try to calibrate where she ranks on some strange scale of self-esteem. I think you only have to look at the myriad temptations of an affluent society. They insinuate themselves into our minds in an unconscious fashion. Luxuries are transformed into necessities, and these necessities become food not only for a hungry body, but nourishment for a soul that is starving.

When I treat people who cannot rein in their own desire to shop and spend money they don't have, I tell them, "Let's suppose a person who spends a lot of money has a gun in front of them. The man holding the gun says, 'I'm going to kidnap you, and if you spend just one penny—I can't help it, I'm mentally sick—I'll shoot you down.' "

The person will stop shopping, no? You bet!

If they can stop shopping because they're in front of a gun, then they can do it without a gun being aimed at them. So shopping is not a medical problem. Sometimes people don't give a damn about their behavior. That's the simple truth.

Another simple truth: people who exhibit terrible or self-indulgent behavior aren't necessarily mentally sick. A mentally sick person will jump from a building or laugh in front of a gun. A mentally sick person can eat glass. But a person who spends too much money is not mentally sick. She is just simply spoiled.

This is what I told Sally. I knew she wouldn't love me for it, just as I knew it wasn't easy for her to hear this. But there was still a chance, however slight, that Sally could salvage her home and protect the money set aside for Sharon's education.

As long as that chance existed, I knew that Sally needed straight talk and not indulgence, harsh doses of reality and not empathy for the "malady" that afflicted her. In my view, she had been treated with indulgence and empathy for too long.

Despite her perilous financial situation, I knew she loved Sharon deeply. I realized that only by making her really *feel* her love for her child would Sally have a chance of salvaging not just her house, but her entire future.

When I say "love for her child," I'm not referring to Sally feeling love for "her own inner child," some minuscule version of herself. No, as far as I was concerned "the inner child of Sally Bryant" had been indulged and allowed to behave like a selfish brat for years. That kind of indulgence had resulted in Sally's current crisis.

It took several months and a few dips in an otherwise upward spiral, but Sally made it. It wasn't easy. Numerous talks with her, followed by several meetings with officials at the bank, were required before Sally could persuade them that she wouldn't fail to repay what she owed. So determined was Sally not to lose the house, she took on a second job. Sharon, as well, had taken an after-school job. The officials were convinced, but Sally was warned that this was her last chance.

The happy news is that her house was saved, and her daughter has just completed her second year in college.

The techniques I recommend in the chapters devoted to craving cigarettes and food are also applicable to the chronic spender. Whatever the craving, breaking the habit can save your life.

This you can accomplish. Should you be seized by an emotion so strong that you feel as if you absolutely must go out and shop, even if it means spending money you do not have, remind yourself of the words that are at the root of everything I've written:

> **What you're thinking,
> this is what your life will be.**

A Lazy Boy Doesn't Necessarily Mean a Sick Boy

It is estimated by some studies that more than 50 million Americans have problems that fall into the category of learning disorders—50 million! According to the United States Department of Education, 20% of all students have a learning disability, while the fact is that only 5% have actually been diagnosed.

Of course, there are genuine cases of learning disability, caused by genuine biological impairment. Yet in many cases, I don't think it's a biological disorder at all, but clearly one that falls quite properly into the category of diseases of affluence.

Let me give you a perfect example. A few years ago, a couple came to my office—I'll call them Dora and Jim Weston. After attending an overeating seminar, they shared with me their concerns about their eight-year-old son, Jonathan. Here is their story: Jonathan's teacher, Irene Russo, called, asking them to meet with her at the school. They weren't totally surprised, because for months, Jonathan's report cards clearly reflected his poor performance in school.

The Westons, fearing their son was facing the humiliating prospect of having to repeat the grade, braced themselves for the meeting. But they weren't at all prepared for what the teacher actually *did* have to say to them. Their son, she told them, was suffering from a disorder, a learning disability.

Taken by surprise with the news that their son was suffering from a disease, the Westons listened as Ms. Russo laid out the disturbing details of their son's poor performance. Then, in a decidedly more cheerful tone, she added that this kind of behavior was so common she saw it every day. Fortunately, there was a simple remedy available. His parents had to realize that he was suffering from attention deficit disorder (ADD). With counseling and perhaps even the use of certain medications, Jonathan would be transformed into a better student. A consultation with a psychiatrist, the teached concluded, was absolutely essential.

"It seems we have no other choice," Jim Weston sighed.

Let me say, at the outset, I'm not a psychiatrist, nor do I pretend to be an expert in learning disorders. But I'd heard similar stories from other parents who had arrived in my office in the same state of confusion as the Westons.

But the Westons weren't completely convinced, at least not yet. I remained vaguely optimistic, saying only, "A lazy boy doesn't necessarily mean a sick boy."

"But the fact is, *Jonathan is failing history,*" Mrs. Weston replied. "He probably does have this disorder."

Jonathan's father added, "In any case, Mr. Shubentsov, we've made an appointment with a psychiatrist. We don't know what this damned disorder is, but we have to do *something.*"

Something told me that in this instance the teacher was wrong. Sensing that the boy wasn't as impaired as his parents had been led to believe, I asked the Westons to let me see Jonathan before they went to the psychiatrist. A few days later, when they brought him to my office, I asked if I could talk with him alone.

"Sit down, and relax," I told him. I could see he was apprehensive about meeting me. "I'm only interested in your telling me about yourself. What do you like?"

"Mostly TV," he replied.

"What specifically on TV?"

"Cartoons," he said simply.

"Which cartoons?" I inquired. My tone was matter-of-fact, but I had a slightly hidden agenda.

Then he proceeded to rattle off one cartoon after another, ultimately giving me a huge list of cartoons. Can you imagine? His mind was absolutely normal! It turns out Jonathan didn't like geography; he preferred cartoons.

Later, I explained to the Westons the same thing I've told other parents. While some children may be properly diagnosed as having attention deficit disorder and be in desperate need of all the help and advantages society can offer, in many cases that I've observed—*too* many—it isn't an illness at all. In fact, these are simply cases of indulged children doing their homework wearing headsets, and their eyes fixed on a TV screen. No wonder they don't know history or math or geography!

If a schoolboy doesn't want to pay attention, before they run to a psychiatrist, his mother and father can say, "You're damned lazy. And you're not going to watch TV until you learn history."

Many couples react like the Westons. They immediately think there *must* be something wrong with their child because he doesn't pay attention. I often advise them, "There's nothing wrong with him, for God's sake! Why is he supposed to be immediately sick, simply because he's damn lazy? Before you go to any psychiatrist, look at your child. If your child can remember ten thousand cartoons, with all the names, all the heroes, all details, it has nothing to do with attention deficit disorder. If the boy can remember telephone numbers, memorize the words to every new rap CD, and recite the batting average of every player in the major leagues, it has nothing to do with *any* disorder."

I'm happy to say that Jim and Dora Weston decided not to consult the psychiatrist. I confess, I imagined, with pleasure how displeased that psychiatrist would be with not only with me but with my approach to Jonathan's "problem."

I repeat, it's an approach that isn't appropriate for every child or every set of parents. Many bright children *do* have cognitive problems in specific areas—learning to read or with math, for instance, and *do* require the special counseling that trained experts in ADD can give them. But as I've indicated, far too many children are being lumped into this category.

Similarly, far too many parents are willing to accept their children as being disabled. Why? It's easier to accept, I suppose, than facing the fact that they have lazy children or unmotivated children. It's easier, I suppose, than bearing the guilt of being an ineffective parent, or a lousy parent, or worse, a lazy and uncaring parent. Parents in this affluent society would rather pay someone else to take care of their kids' problems than take the responsibility themselves. Whatever the case, guilty parents and children mislabeled as disabled aren't sensible solutions to this problem.

"I'm Never Satisfied"

Flick the dial. Turn the page. Stop. There it is—sex addiction—another malady that probably can be categorized as one belonging to diseases of affluence.

In my twenty years in the free world, I've heard a great deal about sex addiction. But in my own office, from the people who come to my sessions on cravings and addiction, I've heard from only a few people who say this is a problem in their lives.

Sex is supposed to be pleasurable; otherwise our planet would be damn empty. Because if sex weren't pleasurable, who the hell would have children? The fact is, no one enjoys being pregnant for nine months, and we have children because it's in our genetic program. Humans, animals, fish. Think of the fish who are impelled to travel against the river to spawn and die after sex. Why? It's in their genetic program to do this.

As for human sex, I don't believe in this thing called sex addiction. To me, it appears that when some people don't want to control themselves sexually, they do what millions of other people do: join the ranks of the afflicted, identify with the armies of people who have eagerly wrapped themselves in the mantle of disease.

Rather than owning up to selfish or self-indulgent or just plain lousy behavior, they prefer to see themselves as victims of a medical problem. They just do what they like, not what they're supposed to do. When I hear about this problem, I always tell the men or the women, if they're married, to express their sex addiction with their spouse. Then it won't be a problem at all.

At the beginning of this book, I acknowledged that my approach was unconventional, and I also said that within these unconventional solutions, it was my hope that you would find a thread you could use in weaving the fabric of your own life.

Your life should have a pattern designed by you, one of your own making. If you are grappling with any of the issues arising out of the constellation of problems that make up the diseases of affluence, you now have all the techniques necessary to defeat them. Once and for all.

To combat the diseases of affluence, here are some new messages to give your brain—a new program for the computer that is your mind.

> Only in an affluent society are people so easily convinced, eager in fact, to believe that their problems are medical and not behavioral. For example, only in an affluent society are parents so easily convinced to buy into the notion that their children's behavioral problems, like not paying attention in school, are medical ones or that his mother is mentally ill if she cares more about being thin than her general well-being.
>
> Only in an affluent society are shopping and spending considered forms of illness.
>
> Only members of an affluent society have the money to

pay the cost of negotiating their way through the thicket of experts available to help treat children.

The hidden addictions of self-esteem and public opinion find fertile territory in diseases of affluence. Be vigilant and make certain they aren't at work, even unconsciously, as you wage war on these kinds of problems.

Think about it! Is this a Mad Russian's perspective? Or is it common sense?

In this chapter, I've tried to provide a method of opening the door that locks you in the rut of certain kinds of self-defeating behavior. Now you have the set of keys.

In the next chapter, I will be at your side as you open the door and make your escape. I want to take at least part of the journey with you as you put some of these ideas into practice. On New Year's Day, we all promise to turn over a new leaf. In this case quite literally, turn over the leaf of this page, and we'll take the first steps into a new world and a new kind of freedom.

Chapter 11

I Shall Not Want

Living in the Soviet Union was not a matter of choice. I was forced to exist in that prison of a country because of stringent rules forbidding its citizens to leave. There were armed guards blocking every possible means of escape.

In time, it became possible to dream about taking my family out of the country. In still more time, the dream became determination. Finally, I was able to make the dream a reality.

In some ways, you and I are alike. Like me, you are now searching for a way to break out of a prison—the prison of living with your cravings. You, too, are determined to make your own dream of escape a reality.

What kept me locked in the hellish world of the Soviet Union were real enforcers and real threats of punishment.

Although you may feel that you too are imprisoned, you are not being kept there by armed guards or by draconian laws that keep you locked under the spell of your craving, be it food or smoking, spending or alcohol. You await no one's permission but your own.

> **W**hat keeps you locked in your prison are your own thoughts and your own vulnerabilities.

You already know the dangers—physical and emotional—of continuing to live with your cravings. You've already promised yourself a hundred times, "I Shall Not Want." Or else you wouldn't be reading this book. That is why I haven't harangued you about the dangers of living under the tyranny of your addiction—whichever one it may be.

Instead, I've shown you how to break through the invisible barriers that keep you bound in the confines of your cell of cravings. I have laid out the path for you to travel so that you can finally live in a world of "I Do Not Want."

I know the prospect of opening the door to a new life for some people is daunting. But there is just one obstacle facing you. And I know it well. Facing the unknown.

For most people, the known always feels safer than the unknown. For some, the known, as unsatisfying or stifling as it may be—whether it's coexisting with the constant gnawing pangs of cravings and addictions, or inflicting the pain of destructive behavior on yourself or your loved ones, or even living in a country where freedom is unthinkable—is preferable to confronting the uncertainties that are part of venturing into the unknown.

Accept Uncertainty as a Companion

You do have a choice: you can be ruled by your cravings and addictions or you can give them up. Naturally, I hope you choose to live without them. If you do, don't be surprised if you experience some moments of uncertainty. Uncertainty is, in fact, part of the very definition of the unknown. It comes with the territory. This I know for sure because in my life I have had more than my share of uncertainty.

I've learned to coexist with uncertainty—sometimes ignoring it, sometimes transcending it, but never avoiding it. So can you.

Still, I know that for each of you reading this book, opening the door to the unknown will mean something different and it may arouse different apprehensions and fears.

It's Not Genetic—It's Your Choice

Looking at the immediate world of your friends and family, you cannot fail to notice the number of people who've chosen the "safety" of the known. I know such a woman. Following her divorce, Claudia Portman began overeating to such a degree that it has grossly distorted her body, and her once beautiful features are lost in the ripples of flesh that hang from her face.

Incredibly, whenever she isn't eating, she's smoking. According to Claudia, a job and a committed relationship would be the perfect antidotes to the loneliness that she insists compels her to overeat and smoke. Yet her obesity intrudes.

Her children are eager for her to visit my office, but she refuses. Why? She won't give them her reasons. But I believe Claudia is fearful of an uncharted course, fearful of leaving her old life, even one driven by the same crippling cravings that offer the dubious comfort of the familiar. Unable to imagine what a new life would be like, Claudia fiercely clings to the familiar, even though it's destroying her. Claudia won't give up her cravings. She won't change. She's too "comfortable."

I don't think people are doomed to gulags of the soul. No matter what you tell yourself, most of these problems are not genetic. You do have a choice. And you have more powers of control than you ever imagined.

Mental Exercises to Help You Climb the Staircase

Imagine that you're opening a large door, and before you there is a long, winding staircase. Each of the steps in this book will take you to another level that, in turn, leads you to yet another set of stairs. As with any act of exertion, including acts of the will, in order to proceed from one level to another, it will be necessary for you to be in shape.

In the following pages, I will give you the exercises and describe the different levels you must reach as you make your way up the staircase. With each step, you'll be closer to another level of strength and resolution. Simply by reading this book, you have already taken a step, and a big one. You're at the *second* landing. I know that's not where you want to be. Not yet.

Level 2: You're on Your Way

At this level, it's important for you to begin the process of changing how you think. In my chapter on stopping smoking, I urged you *not* to replace the cigarette with anything. I asked you to do nothing, absolutely nothing, *instead* of smoking. Just as in the chapter on overeating, I urged you to eat nothing, not even something supposedly as innocent as a carrot, *instead* of something else.

In addition to giving up nicotine entirely or alcohol or chocolate—whatever your particular craving may be—in order to make your way to the third level, you have to give up something else: two conventional ways of thinking.

Do Not Get Caught up in the Tides of Public Opinion

What others say or do, advise or proclaim, has nothing to do with your life. This sounds much easier to accomplish than it really is, for the simple reason that ignoring the currents of public opinion includes so many things. For example, it means:

> Ignoring popular notions of what is beautiful and what
>   is not
> Forgetting clichés like "You can never be too thin"
> Ignoring fads, including miracle diets, revolutionary
>   weight-loss remedies, and buying diet programs
>   that are worthless once you stop using them
> Ignoring new medicines and fads designed to help you
>   stop smoking

Immunizing yourself against all the myths spinning
out of the affluent society

There's more. Ignoring the tides of public opinion also means ignoring the temptation to medicalize each piece of undesirable or socially unacceptable behavior.

Resign from the Cult of Self-esteem

This is the second thought you must abandon, and it's really a product of the first. See this cult for what it is: an excuse machine, that turns out alibi after alibi, to justify or explain behavior that is self-defeating or self-indulgent, terrible for your health, and terrible for your family.

Resigning from this cult is no easy business. Self-esteem is as enmeshed in your thinking as are all the myths of public opinion.

Remember the mental karate I mentioned in an earlier chapter? It can be performed anywhere, anytime. This is a perfect time to begin practicing it. Here are several replacement thoughts that will lead to a more fruitful and fulfilling outcome. These new ideas have an overall design, but you can tailor-make them to fit the pattern of your life.

> Most of the things that plague you, most of the problems that you think are genetic, are not. You aren't doomed. You have the power to change your life.
>
> You don't have to feel victimized.
>
> What you say to yourself in your mind, so your life will be.

Don't overpay with your emotions for things that happened in the past.
Don't dwell on things; change the subject.

As you begin the practice of adding new and powerful
thoughts to your mental karate kit, you'll discover others that directly pertain to your life and to particular situations you're
facing.

They will become like mantras, designed by you. You won't
need to seek out gurus or masters of this or that. *You'll become*
your own guru.

Level 3

Set aside ten or fifteen minutes every day to practice the Bio Energy exercises. In a short time, you won't fail to notice how sensitive your hands are becoming.

But the benefits of tapping into your own supply of Bio Energy
are amazing. You'll experience an awakening of strength. Once
you've located this power of Bio Energy, this power you possess
but never knew you had, your new strength will flow into all the
areas of your life.

Level 4

At this level, in both obvious and subtle ways, your daily life is
being transformed just from the recognition that you possess
powers you never knew about or had not valued sufficiently. Ap-
preciating the values of a tough inner core, the "three Cs" of

intelligence—common sense, creativity, and cleverness—and patience and endurance are necessary for your successful escape from a life ruled by addictions and cravings.

Level 5

You're almost halfway there. I hope you are practicing your mental karate every day. Remember, it isn't time consuming. You don't have to set aside a half hour every day to do mental karate. You don't have to carry a tote bag to work filled with gym clothes; you don't even have to belong to a gym.

Your mind is the gym.

Level 6

Despite all your vigilance, your cravings and addictions, any kind of self-defeating or spoiled behavior can slip back into your life. Sometimes, it seems as if these impulses and desires have lives of their own.

But the fact is they don't. When these desires or cravings return, remember not to dwell on them. Don't even dwell on the fact that they've recurred. If you do, it will only make you more likely to succumb to temptations that you've spent months or years learning to live without.

Change the subject!

You've reached the sixth landing, but you're still several levels away from the top of the staircase. You are still not where you want to be. I say this not to discourage you. Rather, I believe life is a staircase without end.

The essential fact to remember is that if you take one puff, one sip, one bite of the substance you thought you exiled forever, you'll erase all the work you've accomplished in the past.

That is the power of cravings. All it takes is that one—whatever that "one" may be. The familiar quieting, the familiar feeling of unreality, and you're back at the impasse that caused you to approach the staircase at the outset. No damn excuses anymore.

Think of My Book as All the Support You Need

I think each of us should climb a staircase without end. Like the search for knowledge, the search for developing more of our powers, both known and unknown, is one we should pursue as long as we live.

As you climb the staircase to the next level, even if you stumble and find yourself several levels lower than you were before, let my book be a lifeline of support.

Throughout this journey, I've asked you to use your powers of imagination many times. This I do in my sessions as well. This is the last time I will make the request.

So, please. Imagine that my book is the banister you hold as you climb the stairs to each new level, discovering strength after strength. Just as the people who visit my office know they can come again and again if they need support, if you falter or weaken, you can open these pages. You'll find not only the inspiration, but the road map to get you going on your journey, up the staircase, once again.

Earlier, I told you the story of the man who meets an angel in the village. Let me recall it for you. When the man asks the angel who the greatest military leader is of all time, the angel answers, "That old man sitting over there. He is the greatest military leader of all time. He just doesn't know it."

So now *you* know it. Now you know the path to more strength, less dependence, to living without cravings, without addictions, without constant support.

You can make your dream a reality. You can leave the imaginary world of "I Shall Not Want" and enter the real world of "I Do Not Want." Won't that be marvelous? Won't it be great to enjoy your new freedom?

You might be a little surprised you did it.

I'm not. You've had the strength all along. You just didn't know it.